Table of Contents

II. WRITING (& Life)

I. LIFE (& WRITING)

Something We Share,
Something We Don't

THE ONLY PERSON IN my home who thinks about words more than I do is my younger daughter. Here I sit, struggling day after day to find the language I need—because I chose to be a writer and that's what we writers do. And there is my daughter, struggling through her every waking hour to find the right words—because she has an expressive language disability and she has no choice.

For many years, that distorted mirror-image flickered just outside my full attention, like a light in my peripheral vision, present but indistinct. And then one day, writing at my desk, I couldn't think of a particular word, a word that meant precisely what I needed it to mean but also carried some hint of otherness, as so many words do. I wanted to capture the precision and the nuance. I was frustrated with myself for being unable to snatch it from the place where such perfect words hide, obscured by ones that are *almost* the same. And I was enjoying the chase.

In the midst of this, my daughter came home from school, from first grade. After a hug, she said, "Mommy, can I have a glass of...of..."

I waited to see if she would get it. I had been warned that if I kept finishing all her sentences, it would grow more difficult for her to do.

"...of...of..."

"Milk," I supplied.

"Right." She nodded. "Milk."

•

We suspected from early on that something might be amiss but I didn't have the right word for that either. *Just a lot of strange stuff,* was how I thought of it. She didn't crawl until she was over a year. She didn't repeat the sounds I made, in that way most babies do. She took no delight in rhymes, even at three and four. Her speech resisted syntax, seemed incapable of organizing itself into conventional structures. Her utterances had a persistently telegraphic quality. I caught myself supplying words for her as though she were elderly, a little senile.

My daughter was four years old on the day that she and I sat outside on our back step. I was armed with a sheet of white paper, a box of markers, and the determination to make some headway this time. I drew a C. "The C makes a *kuh* sound," I said for the gazillionth time. "*Kuh.* Like *cat.*" I drew a hasty cat face next to the letter. I repeated the word: *cat.* "Now what sound does a C make?"

She looked at me with such genial openness, so unmistakably unpressured to respond, and I understood as I never had before: Everything I had just said—including the fact that I had asked her a question—was meaningless to her.

In a perfect world, she would have been tested the next day and all the appropriate interventions would have started that week, but her preschool discouraged me. She was still well within the range of normal, I was told. Children learn to read at different ages, I was told. My older two children had been exceptionally early readers and I was holding her to too high a standard. I was in danger of *pathologizing* a perfectly "normal," intelligent child.

Intelligent, yes. She was—and she is—extremely intelligent. But "normal"? I really didn't think so, not the way her teachers meant it. Still, I didn't rush her off to be evaluated. Who was I to argue with the experts? And I wasn't in such great shape myself back then, subject to crippling bouts of depression and anxiety after a late pregnancy loss. My confidence in my own judgment was low. Maybe I *was* wrong. Maybe I *was* seeing gloom and doom everywhere. Maybe I *was,* as the school implied, being somehow unfair to my child.

And anyway, wouldn't it be nice to think they were right?

The months crept by, while my concerns about both of us ebbed and flowed. Her development; my emotional health. I would speak with her teachers, and they would tell me to calm down. I would tell myself to calm down, then have a panic attack about something else. I would convince my husband that there was a problem, then turn around and tell him I was just taking my anxieties out on her. My daughter was five before I made real progress in addressing either of our situations to any real effect.

That fall, she entered kindergarten and I began attending a fiction-writing workshop—picking up on a pursuit I had let fall away for many years. As soon as I started writing again I felt the potential for an internal, emotional balance that had long eluded me. Situating myself among words, arranging them, feeling them flow through me as I conveyed my understanding of the world, brought a profound comfort and a sense of new purpose to my life.

My daughter's kindergarten experience was a different story, though. While I discovered a welcoming home in language, she encountered only barred doors. By November, her school was ready to allow for the possibility that something was "atypical" in her development. They thought that she probably should be tested, after all.

We parents, we shine our children up like jewels to highlight what is strongest, most capable in them. Even with all my anxieties, I had been doing it for years. Finishing her sentences, translating her telegraphic utterances. Smoothing her way, trying to. Smoothing her into a different child. Polishing, polishing. Not knowing it, not really, until I watched her testing through a one-way mirror, the process reversed, the glowing, smooth layers stripped back, the rough edges, the fault lines revealed.

We were told that she had an array of language-related disabilities, including an almost complete lack of phonemic awareness, the quality that enables people to distinguish sounds from one another, the quality that makes you able to understand that the word cat is comprised of three sounds. *Kuh-ah-tuh*. It was going to take extraordinary measures for her to learn how to read, endless interventions for her to converse effectively. And a lot would depend on her, we were told. On how hard she would work.

That was fourteen years ago. In the time since, our respective relationships to language have been ever more clearly defined. I began publishing stories in 2003, went for my MFA, started teaching, and have now published books, while my daughter's travels through school have revealed more and more linguistic hurdles she needs to clear. The list of her challenges is long, the ways in which each seems to strengthen the power of the others, fiendish.

And we now define ourselves, both of us, by our relationship to language. Ask me "What do you do?" and the answer is "I'm a writer." Ask my daughter the same question, and the answer is "I go to a school for kids with learning disabilities."

Something we share; and something we don't.

When my books sold, in 2008, I waited to feel the joy that famously accompanies such news, and it never arrived. I was glad for the sale, but in a decidedly muted way. Everyone else seemed so ecstatic for me, while the whole thing had nothing to do with what would really bring me joy. "There's only so happy I can be," I told close friends. "This doesn't make my child's problems any better. It's just something good that happened to me."

The unspoken phrase: *and that can never happen for her.*

What if we were talking about a sport? What about the woman who decides to become a professional runner just as she learns that her daughter will always walk with a cane? What about the trophies she collects? Are they displayed on a shelf? Hidden away? Does her daughter wait for her, cheering, at the finish line? Or does the mother extinguish her own dreams, for fear of saddening her child?

Sometimes, I feel as though I have stolen something that by rights belongs to her. That there is a certain reasonable quotient of pleasure from language to which each of us is entitled, and I took her share, leeched it off of her somehow. Saved myself when I should have saved her. I wept when my galleys arrived, not for joy as we authors are scripted to do, but from a terrible deep sorrow, a grief in me that glistens perpetually with guilt.

That's not of much consequence, though. Ultimately, it doesn't matter what I make of this imbalance of ours. It matters what my daughter makes of her life. Now. Later. My role is a supporting one in her story, though I wish that it weren't. I wish I could sacrifice everything to make her life easier. Because in that story, the one in which I star, my computer bursts into flames and the pages of my books dissolve, the words dancing their way toward my child, who inhales them deeply, allows them to fill her, and easily, easily breathes them out.

But my daughter is the heroine here, heroic indeed as she battles the forces that have senselessly weighted her with these struggles. And I am a writer who has faced, again, again, the painful irony of what I do, and has chosen, again, again, to do it anyway.

"I think I should write a novel for kids your age," I told her one day when she was twelve, thinking, I suppose, that she would feel more included in the work I do, maybe trying to demonstrate that I can amend my inclinations to suit her reading skills.

She shot me a fast, piercing look, and shook her head. "No way," she said. "I'm the one in this family doing that. I claim it. The novel writing thing for kids."

And *there* it was. Briefly. That joy I never otherwise feel. Joy, because whatever I may perceive as *mine* not *hers*, my daughter rejects the notion that everything pleasurable about language belongs to me. Joy, because she has no hesitation in staking her claim.

"I look forward to reading it," I said. "It's all yours."

And I returned to my keyboard, once again.

The Dark Ages: Before I Wrote

IT'S STRANGELY EASY FOR me to forget now how miserable I was over the period of many years when I so, so wanted to write, but could not. My late twenties, my thirties, a time I don't like to think about, much less talk about, not because doing so brings back the unhappiness but because I am embarrassed.

You see, I wasn't nobly unhappy, or quietly unhappy. I wasn't graciously unfulfilled, strategizing with my husband in reasonable tones about possible changes I might make. I was a tantrum-throwing mess. I was a shoe-hurling, pan-slamming, screaming—literally screaming—nightmare. Not all the time, not even frequently; but regularly, and memorably, for sure.

There was a hotel room in Aspen, a family vacation, my three children motionless as I railed. "I hate everything, everything. I hate everything. I just can't take it anymore. I hate everything, absolutely everything!"

I don't know why the dam broke there, on that mountain, that day. I don't know why it broke in my own kitchen on seemingly random afternoons, or in the car on otherwise unremarkable Saturdays.

But this I do know: I did not hate everything. I hated myself. A lot. I so, so, so, so wanted to write. *I so, so, so, so wanted to write.* I had wanted to since taking a creative writing class in college, at the age of nineteen. I had discovered then how powerful and oddly soothing an act it could be for me to make stories up and type them onto the page. I dreamed of making it my career. And yet, for fifteen years, more than that, every time I made a start, I stopped. Not because I disliked the result. I thought I might be pretty good if I could just keep going, but I didn't keep going. I quit. I always quit. And I didn't understand: How could a person simultaneously want to do something so much and be the only thing standing in her way?

For so long, that question seemed to belong to me and me alone, the way my eye-color does, the way my profile does, the way a blood-type once learned is a fact about oneself, immutable. This was my personal, solitary dilemma.

I don't remember ever using the term "self sabotage" to describe this phenomenon until after it stopped being my greatest skill. In fact, I remember a sensation of such infinite unhappiness that very likely I would have rejected anything as compact as a single term to describe it. And I remember slipping from wanting to write to wanting only to *stop wanting* to write, for the longing not to outlive the possibility.

It's been many years since I felt anything like the rage I used to feel at my own inability to follow through. I have never, not even momentarily, been as angry at anyone else as I was at myself for all that time. I have never been as confused by anything as I was by the prison in which I had myself caged. It takes work now to remember the intensity of those feelings, but once I do…I don't entirely understand how I survived such unhappiness, so much self-directed wrath.

Those were terrifying times for me. Not because I thought I would hurt myself—I was spared that particular fear. But because I *knew* I would never be happy, and I knew that I would never be able to be gracious in my sorrow. And I knew—*I knew!*—that this particular misery was mine alone.

But I have since learned how wrong I was about the singularity of my self-sabotage. It turns out that a lot of us subvert our own desires, particularly our ambitions. It is easier for me to see this after the fact, when suffering no longer turns my gaze ever inward. So many of us don't let ourselves have what we want. We don't even give ourselves a chance to try, staying caught in this hellish place of knowing our dreams and being the obstacle to any chance of their fulfillment. And so we live our days in a relentless double-bind.

It's true that I don't like to talk about those times. But now, painful as the memories are, I find that I very much don't want to abandon the woman I was. I don't want her erased from my narrative, her anger and her many failings buried in a blizzard of smiling selfies: *Late Bloomer Poses With Second Book.*

When my second book came out, summer 2014, four years after my first, the phrase reentered my daily life. *Late Bloomer.* I remained a phenomenon—though not such a rare one—because my career began when I was already middle-aged. It's something that strangers knew about me and asked about at conferences, at book clubs, on Twitter— and so on. And in 2010, with publication of my first book, I talked about the experience a lot.

I spoke of my surprise and joy at having a book contract at forty-six, a story collection at forty-eight. A second act. A reinvention. And, with occasional mention of some emotional blocks, I hinted that my three children and their practical needs were the main obstacle to my writing life. "Yes, I was home with my kids full-time for more than fifteen years."

I participated in a narrative, crafted in large part by the subtle pressures of the optimistic story that I understood people wanted to hear, maybe even that *I* wanted to hear, a story less about process than product, less about reality than image, less about empathy than encouragement.

But from one book to the next, something changed. I've grown (even) older and have also grown more secure in my professional identity. And it worries me now that in my rush to be a best-case-scenario role model, I may have made it all look easier than it was, turning what were significant psychological issues into everyday practical problems, like a lack of child care, like having three kids with different vacation schedules—all of which are genuine demands and distractions for any aspiring writer, but far from the true story of what pushed my professional achievements into my middle years.

Not that there is one true story of why I couldn't write with any steadiness until nearly forty, and then why I could. My silence is a prismatic fact, multi-faceted, reflecting emotional issues; fears of speaking my "truth"; underlying conditions such as ADD; family pressures I am still sorting through. My emergence lacks a single simple explanation, only the hard work of years of therapy; the shock of seeing my fourth decade pass, mortality seeming more real; the death of a parent whose very existence seemed to inhibit me; treatment for my ADD; and more, of course, some known to me and much not. It would be nice to have a single key to so dramatic a shift in my capacities, if only to be able to share it in the hope of helping others to become unlocked, but I only have hints and inklings, answers that briefly seem compelling and complete—each one—until I remember another explanation equally thorough, equally true.

Though one fact does come shining through: I did not just need to clear my schedule in order to write. I needed to completely rebuild myself. And it was painful. All of it. Painful, when I wouldn't let myself write, and painful too when I began, when I stuck with it and discovered that the demons of self-sabotage are tenacious and cruel. Painful until it gradually, so, so gradually, became less painful, bit by bit.

And now it isn't painful. I have my bad writing periods, but I'm no longer filled with the kind of self-loathing I harbored back in the bad old days, the Dark Ages, as I have come to think of them. I no longer yell and scream—really, ever. I haven't for years. I can't remember the last time I talked about hating my life, nor the last time I smacked a cooking pan onto a counter with such force that my hand ached. I don't feel now as though I am in some kind of constant battle between my own dreams and my need to subvert them.

I'm doing okay.

This is the point in such essays at which I usually begin to draw some kind of lesson from what I've described. And if there is one here, it's this: I am emphatically *not* an example of someone who first was too busy with her kids to write, and then finally wasn't too busy with her kids to write, so wrote. I am an example of someone who was a complete head case, blocked, miserable, wasting days, years, despairing, depressed, mistreating the people around me, mistreating myself, certain that in old age I would feel a regret so keen that I feared that emotion more than I feared eventual death.

All of which is to say, if you are in anything like that kind of shape, if you are blocked for years and years and years, you are still not disqualified from achieving your goals.

But, to be honest, I am not writing this to send that message into the world—though if it's helpful to someone, I'm glad.

I'm writing this piece because for all that I craft fictions I am a devotee of truth. And recently, as I've looked over my prior writing about being a so-called "late bloomer," I have felt a disconnect between the *rah, rah, you can do it* tone, and the sorrow that consumed me for so long—and still does when I think of those years—sorrow over the decades when I couldn't let myself do what felt so urgent to me, and when I handled that badly. And when I saw myself as my own enemy—because I was.

I no longer want the record sanitized, this story of mine, replete as it is with good fortune, to be recast as only a happy narrative, or as one in which everything fell into place with no damage done. You can't be that frustrated for so long, nor that filled with self-loathing, then emerge without sustaining injury. And to the extent that anyone's paying attention, I don't want to give the impression that beginning a career twenty years after you'd hoped is a simple or painless experience for anyone.

The odds are that if you know someone who has "bloomed" late, that person is carrying serious grief over time gone by. As much as every late bloomer's story can seem like a happy one, it is almost certainly something more. If you stop long enough to ask what lies behind the eventual success—of whatever kind, of whatever degree—you are likely to find a well of pain that may be obscured by relief and gratitude, and possibly, too, by the subtle pressure of other people's needs to see the positive outcome to the exclusion sometimes of much else. You may find a far more interesting story than the one you think you know.

But that's hardly true only of late bloomers.

And that is why I wrote this essay, and why I write the sort of fiction that I write, the sort that earns itself adjectives like "brutal" and "sad." Because nobody's life is simple. And I want to tell this truth: Nobody, no matter what gifts they are given and what joys they embrace, nobody comes out of life wholly unscathed. Everyone has an important, and yes, very often a painful story to tell—whether they choose to share it or don't.

And who knows, maybe that is the simplest explanation, after all, for what kept me so silent for so long. I wanted to tell the truth, and I was afraid of what would happen if I did.

But then I did. And life improved.

There's a moment toward the end of my novel when my narrator, detecting in her husband vestiges of the many people he has been, the boy, the man she married, the man by then in his fifties, wonders, "How was it that any one of us could walk across a room, without our own multitudes tripping us up?" She concludes, "Maybe none of us could."

Of all the lines that I wrote in the book, this one rolls through my thoughts every day: *Maybe none of us could.*

And then: *Maybe none of us should.*

My Default Man

My default man is a bit passive, and he's a good guy, solid—or anyway he seems to be, though he's prone to sexual straying now and then, which argues against that first impression; but the guilt, it tears him up. He's late forties, early fifties, good-looking in an aging-athlete-wearing-glasses kind of way. And he is married. Or he has been married, but screwed it up somehow. Or he has been married but his wife left him for someone a little less dependable, a little more exciting. Because—that occasional sexual indiscretion aside—he is dependable, arguably to the point of being dull. And he's a good father too—to daughters especially, with whom he has that relationship where they know him a little better than he knows himself, which makes him appear to be sheepish in a lovable way. Daughters who say things to him like, "Oh, Dad. You poor old fool." Because he's really just a big befuddled softy inside. And he has a one-syllable name, often one that involves a "k." Jack. Hank. Mike. He's kind of a big lunk is the truth—which also ends with a "k"—and you can't help but like him even if you wish he'd take a little more control of his life.

And there he is, every time I sit down to write. Waiting for me. Bill. Joe. Dick—if it weren't for the need to explain why anyone named Richard would choose to go by Dick, especially this guy, who emphatically would not. He is there, fully-formed, and ready to be kicked around a bit by the women in his life, even as he passively slips into a bed or two that he probably should avoid along the way.

And I, at my keyboard, am dismayed to find him there. Because for all that he seems so passive, so close to bumbling at times, it turns out he is tyrannical with me. A fool for every other woman in his life, he is my master, outsmarting me perpetually, insisting not so much on my attention as on my collusion in keeping him front and center in my work.

I don't know from where he came. I used to have a default woman, but she was pretty clearly me. Every time I started a story, there she'd be. To rid myself of her I put myself on a short-term diet of writing stories only from a male point of view. I hoped that would teach me to grow better at making people up—as opposed to unintentionally reproducing myself on the page, though a wispy, unbelievable version of myself. And it was a good idea. That decision helped me write women who aren't me, mostly because when I wrote women as *secondary* characters I felt freer to give them characteristics that weren't mine. (Ah, ego!) But then, in my place, *he* turned up. Whoever the hell he is.

He isn't my father. I should just get that out there. And he isn't my husband. Nor either of my brothers. He isn't any man I know. I have been dealing with him for many years at this point and believe me I have tried to trace his origin, and it isn't to be found in human form.

So what is he? Other than an embarrassment and a foil all at once? My best guess is that he's a neurotic tic, and he's a tool. Literally. He is the tool to which I instinctively turn when I start writing and am in my most unintentional state of mind. He is the guy whose sole purpose in "life" is to pull the writing out from my inchoate, creative being—which he alone can do because *something* about him puts me in immediate touch with the wounds from which my fiction writing grows.

But I say that like it's an obvious thing, that writing grows from wounds. So I should add, I make no claim that everyone's does; but at this point in my life, having written for quite a while and having gone through many years when it was impossible to write, I am convinced that the reason I write is to occupy what feels like a masterful proximity to those emotions that have caused me most pain. I write to convince myself I can fix those things somehow—or at the very least understand them. I write to heal myself.

I'm not talking about anything conscious here. I have never had the thought: *I could use a little therapy right now, so how 'bout writing a novel instead?* In fact, I barely have a conscious impulse to write. I have instead an itch. A discomfort when I don't write. But not exactly a desire to tell stories. There aren't plots crowding my mind. And I never know what stories I'm going to tell until they are told. But I carry a kind of hunger, or maybe the better image is a barometer that when erratic sends me to my keyboard once again to find calm. And, to find him, which is irritating from a craft perspective—*Lord, can't I come up with another man?*—but probably necessary as a neurotic link to my own creativity, a kind of unassuming doorman to the door that I keep shut against ancient woes.

I suppose he is my imaginary friend, the companion who has been shaped by my earliest psychological distress and whom I intuit, as a child intuits the role of her imaginary friend, has a role in helping me conquer that distress. Maybe he is a transition object of sorts, a security blanket to clutch as I peer into places that frighten me.

But yes, he is irritating from a craft perspective. No one wants people saying, "All of her men are the same!" So I change him. I have tricks for that. Jack becomes Jeremy, and oddly, just the introduction of two additional syllables frees me up—to give him a bad temper, say; or make him a bit cannier than he generally is when he springs fully-formed from my head. Sam becomes Harris, and morphs into a misanthrope. Hank becomes Owen and is capable of torturing his wife into paroxysms of jealousy. No more Mr. Nice Guy. The initial tweaks are small. This odd business of lengthening his name. The forced addition of idiosyncratic gestures. And then, as I gain more control, I can work on the larger stuff, truly change who he is, sharpen that passivity, tame that wandering libido—or not. But in any case, I can consciously craft a character out of the one I unconsciously, reliably produce.

Though sometimes I still see Jack there, and Hank.

I believe that we all have them. Default men, or women, or dynamics, or children, or settings, or conflicts. And I believe, for all my ambivalence about my own, that we all need them, too. These repeated figures, repeated tropes, are the denizens and the pillars of the obsessional, wounded parts of our own creativity—which is to say, our creativity. They remain fairly unchanged over time, as our obsessions and fears are largely unchanging through adult life, set into us early on. So yes, we need them, the repetitions, the familiar scenes and gestures; but then we also need to recognize them for what they are, master them as we move from draft to draft, from the state of intuitive creativity to a state in which the intellect, increasingly guided by intent, kicks in.

This process is much on my mind whenever I begin something new, only to find that he is already there. That guy. My imaginary friend. And I'm learning to give in to him—at first. Let him look embarrassed as he talks about the wife whom he disappointed; allow his daughter to condescend to him in that affectionate way the daughters of my imagination have. Because for all that Jack and Hank and Mike and Bill irk the hell out of me when they first reappear, I recognize that without them I would be stuck, caught in a Scylla and Charybdis of my own: the fears behind my creativity too powerful, the dangers of my intellect stepping in to quell them, too real. I would think too strategically when intuition should still be my guide. I would lose my way back to the source of my writing. Or maybe, without my lunkish, sheepish companion, so essentially dependable, even dull, I would simply lose my nerve.

And so we soldier on, he and I. That's the sort of thing he's best at: soldiering on. Bearing up. Muddling through. And I even let myself enjoy his slightly inarticulate company, his inexplicably irresistible charm—knowing, as I do, that there will be plenty of time to add a couple of complicating syllables later on.

Agoraphobia, Writing, and Me:
Fear and Laughing at Canyon Ranch

In January, 2003, I got in my car and drove a few hours to a luxury spa—Canyon Ranch, in Massachusetts. I'd never been to a spa before (nor have I been since), but that unaccustomed indulgence was the least of what was going on. At forty years old, I was the mother of three children, the wife of one very understanding man, and I was an aspiring writer. I was also a recovering—I hoped—agoraphobic. For eighteen years I had been terrified to leave my home. I had done it, in the course of raising my kids; in the course of the law school years I put in between marriages; in the course of dating the aforementioned husband I'd been married to for eight years by 2003—and in the course of attending a weekly writing workshop in Philadelphia over the preceding eighteen months. So, no shut-in, I. Except for the other seventy-five percent of the time, when I stayed inside, experiencing the crippling panic attacks that almost invariably followed those necessary outings.

Forty-one minus eighteen is twenty-three. At twenty-three I married for the first time and around that time, the panics began. At twenty five, I had my first child, giving me a semi-plausible pretext for staying tethered to my home. And tethered. And tethered. Those few days in the bizarre atmosphere of a spa—hardly adventure travel, I know—constituted the first trip I had taken on my own since 1976, the first time in all my forty years that I'd stayed in a hotel room by myself.

It was an Event. Not just for me, but for my husband and children.

For my mother and my siblings. For the few friends close enough to understand the significance of Robin Out Alone, on the road. And it was a trial run—necessary because the writing thing was getting serious. I wanted to apply to a low residency MFA program, to send out the forms that had been buried on my desk for over a year. But if going to the grocery store reliably resulted in an emergency call to my shrink…

True, I had improved over 2001, 2002. I had worked hard to build my tolerance for being out in the world, but I was shaky still. Very shaky. And I so, *so* didn't want to begin a program only to quit from fear. I knew it would devastate me to come that close to a goal and then disappoint myself again. I was having a hard enough time forgiving myself for those eighteen years of dysfunction; I didn't need another failure on the list.

On the throughway that day, I had a Counting Crows CD on an endless loop, and I was caught in an endless loop of my own. Giddiness, and then unmistakable grief over time gone by, followed by tears of joy, and then giddiness again. I was so proud of myself, even as I was aware of how absurd it was to be moved to tears by my ability to go to a luxury spa. Because with every minute, every mile, I wasn't just driving toward the possibility of an hour-long massage, I was driving toward my adulthood. A little late. But I was.

The emails I wrote home that week were *hilarious*. Or anyway, I remember them that way. They were also endless, thousands of words in each. Accounts of my "adventures" at the Ranch. Much of the comedy was easy—pot-shots at myself for being so uncoordinated, such a disaster at anything remotely athletic, the woman in the back of the aerobics class who trips herself trying to remember which way is "left." And then there was the personal trainer who, as I lay upside down on an enormous inflated ball, dizzy, nauseated, worrying that I might throw up, began for reasons of his own to recite a declaration of love from *Romeo and Juliet*—words that for one mad, disoriented moment I thought were directed to me. (They were not.) The Tai Chi teacher who stood alone with me under snowy hemlock trees, instructing me to picture my "genitals," while holding a "ball of energy" in my hands…

and then, while I struggled not to collapse in giggles, assured me he was picturing his own…The far wealthier-than-I, far better dressed, far better coiffed (which is to say coiffed at all) women discussing over dinner the Canyon Ranch "gas problem" brought on by all the fiber one is forced to eat…Time fades the humor, but in memory these were free-flowing, clever, well-timed accounts, all of them starring me, the clueless, clumsy heroine of her own personal mad-cap comedy.

Now, twelve years later, I am not exactly known for my comic flair. I am a chronicler of grief, a cataloguer of losses. According to the critics, I am "brutally honest" about the "harsh realities of life." I kill off my characters like so many kitchen ants. When I hear from readers it is as often as not to detail just where they were when they started sobbing over some piece of work of mine. (Subways are most common, coffee shops get second place.) I have written the occasional funny piece, but it's surely not what anyone who knows my work first recalls at the mention of my name.

And in fact, up there at long-ago Canyon Ranch, whatever hilarity I dispensed in my daily dispatches home, the "real" writing I was doing at night, a bottle of Jameson's predictably enough by my side, was serious, wistful, oh, and overwrought, directive, written to impress, and, you know, pretty bad. The world was an unhappy place and I was a miserable woman. For all the explosive joy in my email life, for all of my effortless ability to laugh at myself in those missives, I was all about The Tragedy when I *tried* to write. And it was a slog.

In the movie version of this episode in my life, a famous author also staying there—we meet in the sauna, I think—asks to see my work and when I show her those leaden pages, breaks it to me that I have no talent…until she glimpses the emails. "Why, you're just trying to do the wrong thing! You aren't a 'serious author,' at all. You're a comic genius!" And a star is born…

But in reality, the quality of my pages played no role in determining what I would write during the subsequent years. Maybe because I wasn't exactly writing to be read. I was writing to be heard, which is not at all the same thing.

When I look back now, I don't only see those two entirely different streams of words I produced. I see two me's—as clearly as if I had in fact been two different women at the time. How perfect that it was January, the two faces of Janus overlaid with those of Comedy and Tragedy. The irrepressible author of laugh-out-loud emails, looking forward, giggling with every word, dancing under a newly detected light at the end of the tunnel—because she believes that she has done it at last, has vanquished the monster of emotional illness that has kept her hidden her entire adult life. While the other author, fragile and mournful still, embodying the damage of all that fear and loss, struggles, tentative and self-conscious, to put to page why her sorrow mattered, why it had to matter, what she has learned, what she might share.

When my first book came out, one of the most instructive things anyone said was in a nasty one star review. "I don't know why she thinks anyone would want to read anything this depressing," the reviewer opined. And I realized only then how little I had thought about what anyone else what might want to read. I had written what I had to write. Those Canyon Ranch emails were fun and all, but that other woman, the grieving one, she and I had unfinished business.

Perhaps I am thinking of that trip now because after years of steady work I am between fiction projects. I'm not under contract for anything. I'm back to writing for nobody but myself. And it's not clear to me that I know who I am these days. At least not when it comes to the work. My story collection and novel were part of one long process for me, a particular me, that chronicler of grief, cataloguer of losses. The forces that had kept me hidden needed exorcising—or something like that. I hesitate to pin down too neatly what that gust of need was in me. The "why" of all those words.

But I know that the "why" has changed. Because I am changed. I still have my sorrows, but I no longer define myself by them. I chafe now when I imagine myself once again sitting at my keyboard to type out my hard-earned expertise on the finer points of emotional pain.

And so I have no idea what comes next. I have no idea what kind of writer I am. I only know I am not the writer I have been. It can be discomfiting. Starting over. But maybe that's just what we writers do—every time, with every blank page.

In the movie version of *this* era of my life, I go out to the garage and unearth the hard drive on which all those emails have been waiting to be reread, and I manage to tap into them somehow. I sit among the boxes and the bags of clothes, devouring every word—and I laugh out loud, just as advertised. Though maybe I also discover that they aren't quite as unrelentingly hilarious as I have long believed. Maybe they are even a little poignant, a telltale line toward the end of each: "So far I'm doing okay, fingers crossed" or "Nothing worrisome yet. I'm holding steady."

How could there not have been that nod to my reality?

But yes, far more vibrant is the voice of the other woman I was that week. The irrepressible woman who saw humor everywhere she looked, who cast herself in the role of ditzy heroine. The one who must have believed that this day of not defining herself by early sorrow would eventually arrive.

"Dear All," she wrote to her worried family back home, *"Just try to picture me like this…"*

Father Chronicles: Embracing Cordelia

WHEN I WAS A girl, my father would invite me to his study on the third floor of our house, take down the great white leather-bound volume of *The Complete Works of William Shakespeare*, and open it to *King Lear*. We would read much of the opening scene aloud, he playing Lear of course, and I cast as first one daughter then the next, reciting the elaborate protestations of love from Regan and from Goneril and then, finally, Cordelia's fateful speech:

"*Good my lord,*
You have begot me, bred me, loved me: I
Return those duties back as are right fit,
Obey you, love you, and most honour you.
Why have my sisters husbands, if they say
They love you all? Haply, when I shall wed,
That lord whose hand must take my plight shall carry
Half my love with him, half my care and duty:
Sure, I shall never marry like my sisters,
To love my father all."

What followed then—in my father's study, not in the play, though one could argue the distinction—was a lesson about the coldness Cordelia displayed, a discussion of why she should have just played along, of how hurtful that must have been to her father.

It was a position with which I was quick to agree.

•

I was a skinny child, slight, pale, looking a bit like Tenniel's Alice. I was no Cordelia, no speaker of truths, no smasher of illusions, no expert even on what illusions there might be to smash. I was in love with my father, who encouraged a kind of romantic connection between us. And being in love with my father meant inhabiting a world of make-believe so elaborate and so apart from reality it might as well have included a Queen of Hearts, a Cheshire cat, a March Hare, King Lear, and Cordelia, too. I had little sense of what made sense. I was too happy at having my father's attention to understand what else of his I was receiving—and of course, I was also too young.

I did not know that the romance between us was a classic way alcoholics relate to their children, a crossing of boundaries that would damage me for years. I did not know that this sort of attention, the sort that served an agenda of his, was perhaps not a perfect substitute for such things as his knowing what grade I was in that year; and I did not know that he did in some way know all this, that the knowledge of his own shortcomings lurked both uncomfortable and unattended in his heart.

I was thirty-nine when my father died, and within three weeks after his death I began to write—for real, as I like to say. I had made attempts over the years, and had even had the sort of success that should have spurred me on—flattering workshop receptions in college, encouraging teachers. But I had always quit before completing anything that felt finished to me—as finished as fiction ever feels, which is never quite finished, just finished enough. I never let myself reach finished enough. Until my father died, at which point the floodgates opened and my work found its way into the world.

The title of my first book, *If I loved you, I would tell you this*, is the opening sentence of a story I wrote in 2006 when our new neighbor built a fence in a location he was technically entitled to use but that we had believed was part of our property. The fence greatly diminished the use and beauty of our home's entrance, and I found the whole episode staggering, in no small part because our request by the end was only that he move it six inches. His response was to take the yarn my husband had used to show where that shifted line would be—yarn accompanied by a very polite note—ball it up, and throw it onto our driveway with no further comment. He not only did what he was legally entitled to do, he did it with spite.

My initial impulse was to write an essay on the subject. I almost never use events from my own life in fiction, so memoir seemed the way to go. The essay was to be on the question of entitlement, addressing how much of life and personal interaction turns out to be defined by the question of who feels entitled to what. But at some point, it began to feel labored, a little over-thought. I lost interest, and then, in an uncharacteristic move, I decided to write a short story about the experience instead, a story in the form of direct address from one character to another. The first line I wrote was: "*If I loved you, I would tell you this.*"

The point of that line, of the whole story really, is that taking the time to work something through with someone who has hurt you, rather than just giving up, is itself a loving thing to do. And that a relationship that precludes such discussions and such mending along the way, is a relationship that also precludes an intimate, trusting love.

My relationship to my father was indeed tragically disintimate. Replete with ritualized protestations of adoration from both sides, it lacked this single crucial aspect: the possibility that painful disclosures might also be constructive and loving ones.

When my stories were collected, my working title was "Yesterday's News." I liked the way the phrase captured both the sense that the stories dealt almost entirely with the process of recovery from a loss or trauma; and also that it was a play on a way that older women, so often central to my work, are demeaned.

But the title was a non-starter for my publisher as it violated the number one rule of titles: Don't give reviewers ammunition. Don't make it easy for some nasty critic to say: "These old-fashioned stories really *are* yesterday's news!" (Which, as an aside, answers the question of why no one ever calls a novel *This Piece of Shit Book.*)

I won't list the dozens of title possibilities we canvassed, but I was the first to suggest "If I loved you, I would tell you this," and also the first to decide it was a terrible idea. What a mouthful! I couldn't imagine saying it out loud every time someone asked me the name of my book. But, for better or worse, my publisher was in love, and so set about convincing me of its virtues, in part by showing me the degree to which the theme of speaking the truth, of speaking difficult truths, of lives turning on the question of who discloses what hard truth to whom, dominate the book, central to nearly every story.

There are two kinds of obsessions for a writer. There are the ones of which we are aware—which for me include such things as interiors of houses, representational art, and on a somewhat deeper level, loss and recovery from loss. Betrayal. Redemption. And then there are the ones of which we are unaware—until somebody points them out. These can feel oddly embarrassing, as we learn that we have unintentionally exposed a deeply personal vein.

Rereading my stories through the lens of that one line, "If I loved you, I would tell you this," made me feel stupid, obvious, and yes, embarrassed. That reaction has faded, and I've recovered my ability to read the book without that particular theme blinking in red lights when I do, but, at the time, the revelation that I was consistently and unknowingly hitting on one particular theme was an unsettling one.

It took several years after that for me to begin another project that "took." There are myriad reasons for that, but a feeling of self-consciousness certainly played a role. I was under contract and I felt watched, as if my editor had nothing better to do than wonder where my pages were. And I felt too a different form of self-consciousness, as though I knew too much about myself. With each work that I began I would either avoid all issues of truth-telling and disclosure, or I would see them emerge and abandon the work, knowing that with its heart revealed to me, I would no longer write from my own.

When I finally embarked on the novel that "took," I convinced myself that I had banished the subject of prohibited speech. The story takes place long *after* the secret of an affair has been revealed, and is overtly about another of my obsessions, one that hadn't been explored as thoroughly in my stories: the subject of betrayal, not just marital or sexual betrayal, but betrayal of all kinds. When people asked me what the book was about, I always described it as the story of a couple trying to recover from a confessed betrayal, and of friends dealing with a betrayal as well. To clear the book even more thoroughly of all secrets, in the first sentence the narrator discloses to the reader that her husband is going to die. On both a textual and meta-textual level, everything has been told before you're even one chapter in.

But a funny thing has happened in the years since I finished the book. I have found myself rethinking it, and I would no longer describe it as a story primarily about a couple trying to recover from the woman's affair, or friends coping with disloyalty. I would describe it this way instead: "*Life Drawing* is a novel about a woman whose father made many important subjects in her life taboo when she was a young girl. This prohibition on honest discourse so shaped her that she has a shaky hold on the way truth-telling is sometimes beneficial and sometimes damaging, a lack of insight that leads to a tragic end."

And I might quote this line in which the narrator, in response to a conversational awkwardness with her husband, makes a revelation: "*This wasn't my first experience living under a regime of unspeakable subjects. I was well-practiced. After my mother died, my father mandated that she not be mentioned, so by the time my conscious memory of childhood kicks in, I was already trained to short-circuit the flow between my thoughts and my voice.*

"*There were very few ways in which Owen reminded me of my father—at certain points just the idea of any similarity would have horrified me—but in fact both had played this censoring role in my life, rendering my speech a kind of topiary, trimmed and trained and shaped to please.*"

These sentences appear on page twenty-seven, hardly buried in the book.

So how I could not have known that I was back in familiar territory? It seems so obvious, now—the crucial sub-plot of the father forbidding certain speech. How could I not have heard the resonances with my own life?

The best answer I know is that we writers protect ourselves as we work—*when* it is going well. We make ourselves immune to observations and insights that might hold us back; and this blindness can be a mark of a productive writing period. The best of my writing requires a kind of imposed stupidity about what I'm doing. I wasn't able to write a book until I had convinced myself that I'd moved away from this theme; but I am certain that I couldn't have written a book had I *actually* moved away from this theme.

It's a blessing really that we are capable of being obtuse about what we reveal. Remove the unintended obsessional layer from anyone's work, and you almost certainly remove the layer that produces urgency. Read work that lacks urgency, and you will often discover a piece that was over-thought, pre-planned, written to fit a formula or an idea, a piece in which the unconscious obsessions of the author have had no room to thrive. A piece, perhaps, in which the author has too successfully protected herself from exposing herself.

When I think of beginning another book or story now, it is this for which I most fervently hope: Please let me be an innocent as I write, let me not understand the process too well, let me be surprised again at what comes out—even if it is, as it likely will be, the very same thing I have written a thousand times before. Please, allow me to tangle with Cordelia once again, for all the world to see.

House Lessons I:
Aspirational Storytelling

On a sunny afternoon many springs ago, a young man rang our doorbell, clipboard in hand. He looked like every earnest canvasser who had ever come to call, but he wasn't there for my signature. He was there to inform me that the spectacularly unkempt appearance of our house made us likely candidates for a free façade makeover on a new TV show that might as well have been titled: "Wow, Your Neighbors Must Really Hate You."

My visitor grew excited as he waxed rhapsodic about our busted shutters and three-story-high hedge, but I felt more as though I were receiving an unwelcome diagnosis than a gift. I'd spent years convincing myself that the house wasn't really that bad, and now here was this oddly enthusiastic stranger dismantling my delusion. At one point, as he took pictures, I muttered "Lord," and he muttered, "I kind of hate this part of my job." But then, very soon, with only negligible resistance on my part, we slipped from the norms of decent society into another set: the norms of reality TV.

It's a bit like *A Christmas Carol*. One message of Scrooge's big night is that if you behave hideously enough, otherworldly beings will intervene. And today if you step too far outside what society expects of you, the denizens of reality TV swoop in. The extremely obese are fair game, the rampant procreators, the neglectful homeowners lowering the property values of their lovely neighborhood.

I called my husband Richard, who was skeptical—first that I wasn't pulling his leg, and then that we should get involved. But I was already a naturalized citizen of Reality World, and I felt a distinct impatience with his reactions, never mind that they had earlier been my own. How could he be embarrassed, or have doubts? We'd been invited into a realm in which our failings would turn us into stars. And we'd get free stuff. I was adamant, wheedling, nagging. He didn't hesitate for long.

Some tense days later, we learned that the network loved the documentation of our disrepair, but we were cautioned that we were in competition with another house in the neighborhood, a property equally run-down. My son took a practical approach. "I think we should find it and fix it up, weed the place, trim their hedge." We all thought that was brilliant, and never once puzzled over why, if we had it in us to do that in the name of cheating, we couldn't manage to do it on our own property for more conventional reasons. In the end though, we never found the other house. And our investigative drives through streets of monolithically well-tended properties depressed me. It looked so simple, so doable. The mowed lawns. The weeded gardens. The trimmed hedges. We were, I realized, an oddity. The people about whom others must talk, clicking their tongues, rolling their eyes.

"So what's our story?" I asked Richard, the night before our final audition was to be filmed. "How did this happen?"

They are never precisely the same question, of course, the story one tells and what has actually taken place, and in the distinction lies not only the immeasurable gulf between reality TV and reality, but also the seductive thrill of reworking one's own narrative. The story we crafted that night was one of good-natured over-achievers who couldn't possibly do it all. The next day, as the camera rolled, I bubbled over, doing my best to be charmingly ditzy, babbling about how in lives as rife with interest and accomplishment as ours, something's gotta give. Richard gave a mock serious performance as the husband of the zany wife, the man who's just trying to keep up with all the hilarity. And in the end, we stood together, arms wrapped around one another's backs and called out with some heartfelt passion, "Please! We need your help!!"

As for how it had really happened, the busted shingles, the overgrown hedge, that was mercifully irrelevant throughout.

"God, imagine, if they don't take us," I said, as days passed by. "That must be the worst. They tell you your property is a disgrace, then abandon you." And of course that's exactly what happened. The other house won—not because it gave them a better challenge, as I had worried, but because it was in better shape. A less daunting project.

"I'm really sorry," the producer said. "The network loved you guys. They loved your story."

Sure they had. So had we.

As the sun set that evening, Richard and I stood out on the curb, studying our home of fourteen years. I looked down the street at the other houses, neat and tidy, conforming to expectation, the words "All happy families are alike..." crossing my mind.

How had this happened? Really? There were unanticipated losses, grief that enveloped us for years. A stillbirth. A beloved child with special needs. Challenges we never imagined we'd confront. None of it amusing. Nothing like a situation comedy. We'd let go of so many easy assumptions about how our lives would proceed, and in the process we let other things go as well. Gradually, we learned to live a new story, different from the one we had imagined would be ours. Maybe we had even became stronger, doing so. But the evidence of our faltering remained, the façade of our home stubbornly unable to mend itself, obstinately true.

Beside me, Richard sighed.

"Reality's a bitch," I said, reaching for his hand. "Let's go back inside."

Autumn, 1972

MY MATERNAL GRANDMOTHER MOVED into our home when I was ten. Grandma was a tough cookie. Shtetl-born, Lower East Side raised, the second oldest of eight children, seven of them girls, she had the reputation among her own generation as a drill sergeant. She was certain in her own opinions, a woman to whom it had seemingly never occurred that she might be wrong. Her favorite, oft-repeated expression was, "There's a right way and wrong way to do everything," and it was clear into which category her way invariably fell. But she was also a woman of contradictions, unexpectedly tender-hearted, and always likely to side with the underdog, yet someone who hadn't hesitated to smack around her own sons when she thought they'd stepped out of line. A good woman? A bad woman? A complicated woman. And, by the time she moved in with us, a seventy-two year old woman who had been paralyzed from the waist down from spinal tumors for more than ten years, and widowed for most of that time.

As a writer, it's almost inevitable that you will wonder sometimes what made you the sort of writer that you are, what periods of your life, what particular events, what people. It's a strange kind of inquiry because of course there is no definitive answer, but still, there are these little glimmers you can find, moments and exchanges that seem to explain something, if not everything. Grandma's move into our home offers just such a glimmer for me.

•

During the initial years of her paralysis, after her widowhood, she had lived alone, a couple of hours away from us, maintaining more independence than anyone could believe. Her six sisters did her shopping, provided her with constant company, and played other crucial roles in helping her. One of my earliest memories is of watching her wash the dishes, the gravity of her weight against the sink keeping her upright. And she would cook that way too, or sometimes she would do it by pulling her wheelchair up to the kitchen table. She wasn't exactly mobile, but she wasn't exactly immobile either—until something shifted in her damaged spine.

By the time she moved in with us, there was some talk of her continuing to be active in the ways that she had been, but in fact she soon became entirely bedridden—as she would be until her death at nearly eighty-three.

I was ten years old that first day, November 1972, and I was not a happy child. My father, alcoholic and depressive, had been institutionalized for many months in '71, an experience preceded and followed by disorienting chaos in our home. But I remember being giddy around my grandmother's move to our home. It seemed like such fun, so cool to have her there. It was a change in our routine; and maybe the routine of our house was unhappy enough that any change seemed promising. I wrote poems to commemorate the event and I raced my brothers in Grandma's two wheelchairs, and I made a lot of what I thought were very funny jokes about—of all things—an imaginary suitor for her.

Here, an element of self-protective repression sets in, because I don't remember the specifics of this long-running joke of mine. He had a name, he had a spiel—all of it mercifully gone from my mind. But what I do remember, vividly, is the evening my mother took me into the hallway and suggested as gently as possible that I stop. "You know, if Grandma hadn't been in a wheelchair, stuck in her apartment, she might have had a real suitor. She might have remarried after my father died. It may well be a thought that makes her sad, so it's probably not something you should joke about now."

When I remember that moment, so long ago, I feel an array of things—most obviously my own shame, even horror, at my mother's words. I had thought I was being funny, cheering everybody up, when in fact I had been causing pain. It was devastating. And I sense too, even now, the reverberations of a kind of shattering of my foundation and a quick rebuild, a change at a molecular level of who I understood myself to be. No longer someone who could look at another person without wondering what their life was like, but someone with a new curiosity about what people's stories might actually be. Below the surface. Not because I suddenly became a better person, but because I was terrified— and perhaps am terrified still—of again being inadvertently cruel.

The impact of that evening goes beyond this vague notion of having an empathic imagination shocked into me. When my story collection came out, people often asked me why so many of my stories were about older women, women in their seventies and beyond. "I feel a commitment to reminding people that older women are still complex human beings," I would say. A worthy goal? Of course. A lifelong creative penance for having been a little girl who hurt someone by forgetting that fact? Perhaps.

What does it take to write fiction? The answer is as varied as the results that emerge when a hundred million authors sit down to write. What determines our obsessions? The places and people toward which our imaginations are drawn? The questions are both unavoidable and unanswerable. But I suspect that each of our lives is scattered with such glimmers, shimmering shards that provide a glimpse—and that may always remain sharp enough to cut.

AD(H)D I

ON A RECENT EARLY evening, my husband drove nearly four hours, round trip, to fetch my wallet. We were away from our home, but my wallet was still there. The return leg would be after dark, and my vision makes night-driving difficult. He didn't look happy as he set off, but he made the drive, and, considering everything, he did it with remarkable grace.

I say "considering everything" because this is a common occurrence for me, and therefore for him. I don't mean that I leave my wallet two hours away with any regularity, but that my entire life is short on regularity and long on forgotten necessities: lost keys, unpartnered shoes, and so on. I am perpetually defeated by physical objects, often in a panic over something that's gone missing, frequently hurling vivid, heartfelt insults at myself for losing everything that comes into my care.

"How is it possible?" I asked recently about a scarf, while stomping around our home. "I swear to God, I was just holding it, telling myself to remember where I put it. How does this happen to me no matter what?"

"Are you talking about this scarf?" my husband asked, producing it, magician-style from under the couch, where I had looked three dozen times.

A lot of people don't believe in Attention Deficit Disorder, but those who suffer from it do. I suffer from it, and my husband suffers from my suffering from it. Long ago, my father-in-law walked into our messy home and said to me, of his beloved son, "You've broken him."

"I'm sorry," was all I could think to say in response.

Apologies are tricky, though. It was easy enough to apologize to my father-in-law for lowering his son's housekeeping standards— by a lot—but if I apologized to my husband for every inconvenience my ADD causes, we would have little time left to speak of anything else.

And apologies are tricky, too, because it's not so simple to forge and maintain a strong relationship in which one of you is so, well, abysmal, at so much, while the other happens to be, as my husband is, so incredibly good at the very same things. And it's not as if I'm talking about doing calculus or juggling, activities that come up rarely if ever. I am talking about the practical matters of everyday life.

To be clear, he knew what he was getting into. When we met, 22 years ago, my electricity had been recently cut, not because I lacked the funds, but because I forgot to pay the bill, which I had also lost. Shortly before that, it was my phone. After we'd dated only a few times, I called him at his office because, my attention elsewhere, I had driven the wrong way over parking lot spikes, flattening all four of my tires. Our courtship was positively bedazzled with just such episodes—not to mention that he'd seen my apartment in all its chaotic, haphazard, never-been-vacuumed glory. So he was definitely forewarned.

And in fact I was the one who went in blind, completely unprepared for how it would feel to live with someone who, through no fault of his own, seemed perpetually to be showing me up. I was unprepared for the rage I would direct his way every time he fixed something I had broken or found something that I had lost. I had no idea that I would become essentially allergic to his even noticing that I had messed up again—which is like saying I was allergic to his knowing that I have blue eyes.

"Why don't you just let me help?" he has asked, perhaps a trillion times. And for years, the answer, which I couldn't bring myself to articulate was: *Because if I do, it will make my loser status in this relationship official.*

"I don't understand why you're mad at me for finding your keys," he would say.

Because it makes me feel even worse about myself.

There was something else, too. When we met, I was a newly single mother of two small children, ages five and two. For a long time, and from a lot of people, I heard (endlessly, endlessly) about how lucky I was that he had been undaunted by that fact and had taken us on. It seems bizarre now, even to me, how many people said exactly that, with how little sense of how it might make me feel, but in fact it was a constant theme. And they weren't wrong. I was incredibly fortunate, as were my kids. But after enough people said it, I began to feel like some kind of good-deed sacrifice my husband had made, his sad-sack, pity-marriage of a wife.

"I could help you organize your papers, you know. Why don't you just let me?"

Because if I have to deal with one more reason to be grateful, I am going to implode.

So the truth is that he wasn't really forewarned either. Because, though he may have known he was marrying a woman who couldn't maintain any semblance of physical order and whose wandering attention would often leave havoc in its wake, he had no idea that I would be angry at him because of that. Angry and ungracious—as he found my left sneaker, cleaned our clogged gutters, replaced our souring milk, and remembered to pay our bills. The bastard!

But then something in our dynamic shifted.

I know that marriages supposedly don't change overnight, not by common wisdom, but common wisdom doesn't take into account what I like to think of as The Best Day Ever: the day my husband backed one of our cars out of our driveway, and smashed it into our other car, crumpling a decent-sized portion of both. It was a day that ushered peace and tranquility into our lives, the twofer that will live forever in family lore.

I burst out laughing when he told me. But he did not laugh. I rejoiced in spite of the money it was going to cost. He was in a foul temper for reasons having little to do with the money. I was more in love with him than I had ever been before. He was disgusted with himself.

"You really don't see the humor in this?"

"No, I really do not see the humor in this."

Finally, after I stopped high-fiving myself, and he stopped seething (a process that in each case took hours, if not days), we had the conversation.

"You know that way you felt, when the one car hit the other car? Like a complete and total moron?" He winced, but nodded. "Well, that's how I feel half a dozen times every day."

"I understand."

"And you being so good at everything, it sometimes just makes me feel worse about myself."

"I understand that, too. Though clearly I'm not good at everything."

"And really, I think it has something to do with my having had the kids as well, the whole rescue of the single mom thing—"

"Even though I've never felt that way?"

It seemed, in prospect, like an important conversation to have—though once we did, it became obvious that my husband had known about these dynamics all along. He's a very smart man. Of course his ADD-ridden wife felt bad about her ADD. And of course she worried that she'd already come into the relationship as a burden because of the two children she brought with her who weren't yet his. But what was he supposed to do, even knowing that his competence bummed me out? Leave our bills unpaid and not produce my missing scarf from under the couch? Let me storm and wail, when he could see my keys on the counter plain as day?

And where had I thought this conversation would lead? Did I believe that if he better understood me, my husband would stop trying to help me? That he should? It seems like a dead end kind of goal.

The whole episode might well have led exactly nowhere, except that in the process, I came to see that while I was focused on changing him, it was—of course—I who needed to change.

These days, in fiction, the sort of epiphanies where characters suddenly understand what their problem has been all along are out of style. It seems so contrived, so unlikely. But the bar for plausibility is higher in fiction than in fact. Real life can be, often is, implausible—yet true. And I did indeed have one of those sudden moments of understanding, soon after my husband simultaneously wrecked both our cars.

So what did I do?

Reader, I liberated him. I freed him from the cage of perfection in which I held him trapped. I was so neurotically addicted to seeing myself as the screw-up that I had forgotten to see him clearly at all, to notice how rapidly he, too, despised himself for making a mistake. I'd forgotten to understand that he has his own struggles, of a different nature from mine, but no less real, and no less deserving of a helping hand now and then.

It isn't easy to alter a long-term marital dynamic, even after a quickie epiphany, but over time I have gradually stopped forcing him into the role of paragon and started accepting his help, far, far more graciously than I ever did before. I now encourage him to enjoy his competency and the satisfaction of bolstering me where I am undeniably weak. And, perhaps most importantly, I have started reciprocating more, discovering ways in which I might help him—even remaining silent when he says that he "meant to do that," to smack the one car into the other, because he knew it was exactly what our marriage needed at the time.

"I really appreciate this," I said, when he set off on the long drive for my wallet. "It's incredibly nice of you."

"No biggie," he said. "I'll be back soon."

"Drive carefully," I said—biting back the suggestion that he watch out for parked cars.

A Life of Profound Uncertainty

I WOULD NEVER ASK anyone to pity the poor writer her plight. *No one* has to be a writer. Even those people who claim that if they couldn't write they would shrivel, raisin style, because their need to express themselves is so *blah, blah, blah*—even they don't *have* to be writers. They *choose* to be writers. They get to be writers.

Still. While writers don't deserve the sort of sympathy appropriately reserved for people whose difficulties are *not* by-products of a privilege granted them, it's true that being a writer can be a psychically uncomfortable life. "No Whining" makes a fine motto, but there's value nonetheless to understanding why this pursuit feels so difficult at times, why the writer's existence can be so isolating, and even so frightening; and there's value to exploring whether it's possible to restructure one's perspective to make it less so.

"A life of profound uncertainty." That's the phrase I use when questioning aspirants about whether they really want to take this on. And this is what I mean: On any given day, I don't know if I will be able to write, I don't know if I will like what I produce, I don't know whether if I like it by evening, I will like it the next day or discover a hard drive full of dreck, I don't know if anyone else will like it, I don't know if the work will achieve whatever practical goal I have set (publication, for example), I don't know whether, if published, it will find readers for whom it "succeeds," I don't know if any of that will lead to any financial remuneration, I don't know if I will be publicly insulted or lauded for the work I have done, or ignored. I don't know what impact the introduction of other readers, including critics, will have on my own feelings about my work or about my ability to do it, which brings us full cycle to the fact that on any given day I don't know if I will be able to write.

It can be pretty destabilizing, all that not knowing. Pretty damned uncomfortable, too.

I've thought a lot about this in the past few years. Like others before me, I've learned that publication, while welcome, does not introduce any greater level of psychic certainty into the equation. It seems to be close to universally true that after publication the degree of one's insecurity about all things writing-related remains about the same, though the subject matter of the anxieties may be changed. Instead of worrying over getting a story published, you can worry about getting a bad review, or about not appearing on a prestigious list—but you are still worrying.

I have friends whose careers seem like the absolute dream outcome for anyone—and they too are fragile about these *not knowings*. A solitary star on Goodreads can ruin the day of a writer who has won international awards. An unstarred *Publishers Weekly* review can ruin a week. A week of feeling uninspired erases years of productivity, leaving the latest critically acclaimed phenom doubting that he'll ever write again.

I'm hardly the first person to describe this condition, the enduring fragility of highly successful writers. There are plenty of articles about this subject online, and I often see comments, below, that hurl insults at these people, these enviable yet anxious beings. They should get over themselves; they must be terribly conceited if they want universal approval; they need to be tougher; they are ingrates, considering all they have; they should *make it be about the writing* and stop worrying about success; their priorities are fucked up. But those insults fail to take into account how common this fragility is. It isn't an idiosyncratic response that a few narcissistic authors have. It's far closer to being the norm.

Like water seeking low ground, we writers seek uncertainty even in situations where it might make more sense—not to mention, be more comfortable—to latch onto the reassuring knowledge we have gained.

And though writers tend to bemoan this fact—*Why does nothing ever make me feel secure in this pursuit? Grrrrr.*—I'm beginning to wonder if uncertainty isn't actually something for which to be grateful.

I'm not suggesting that writers need to be emotionally unstable in order to write, I have never bought into the notion that psychological struggles make for better art. But perhaps for many writers there is an instinctive recoil from a comfortable state of satisfaction—since it's very likely that a sensation of *dis*satisfaction led to this work. Perpetual uncertainty may be a way of protecting creative restlessness, of guarding against a complacency that threatens creativity.

My own earliest impulses to write grew directly out of a strange interplay between intuition and confusion, with a large dose of ignorance thrown in. For me, writing has always been about trying to make sense of things that I don't understand, and not about certainty of any kind. It has always sprung from a sense of curiosity, precisely from a condition of *not knowing*. My creativity isn't rooted in confidence. It grows from many things, no doubt, but chief among them is a deep, rebellious, and indeed almost hostile stance toward complacency—about anything. It feels like the enemy. And certainty? It closes doors. Ends discussions. Shuts other people out.

Perhaps the real question for those who consider making this pursuit central to their lives is not "Are you ready for a life of profound uncertainty?" but "Are you uncertain enough to take on a life of creative work?"—a question to which the only acceptable answer may be: "I don't know."

On Not Reading

FOR ABOUT FIFTEEN YEARS I barely read a single book. I started life as one of those book-obsessed children, devouring pages, chapters, tomes, series, entire library sections of books. I read voraciously through high school, through college, through…well, that was about it. I graduated college at twenty-four, had my first child when I was twenty-five, my second three years later, my third at thirty-three and I had two pregnancy losses as well. Five pregnancies in ten years. Three little kids. One failed marriage along the way. Two and a half years of law school. A new husband. A child with special needs. A mother twice hit with life-threatening illness. A dying father. And nary an open book in sight—beyond cookbooks and those legal casebooks I tried and tried to read, but surely not because I wanted to. From 1987 or so to 2001, more or less, I left fiction behind.

And maybe not only because I was so busy during those years. In college I had wanted to be a writer, and had thought I would be one, but I soon chickened out of even making the attempt. Looking back, I suspect that reading fiction became too painful for me, too much of a reminder of what I'd been unable to do. I didn't abandon the joy of reading fiction because I had a houseful of children. It is closer to true that I had a houseful of children at least in part because I'd abandoned my other ambitions, chief among them writing books.

In 2003, having reignited that dream, I found myself flooded with embarrassment at an early meeting with my first advisor in the Warren Wilson MFA Program. Part of our task was to draw up a reading list for the semester. He asked me whom I had read. "Well, Virginia Woolf of course. Edith Wharton. George Eliot. Some Borges, in college. Henry James, Flannery O'Connor..." He put his pencil down. "What about contemporary writers?" I bit my lip. Then I remembered something. "A friend of mine gave me a book by someone called Lorrie Moore. Short stories. And I've read a story also by someone called Alice Munro. And...And a novel by someone called Francine Prose..."

I rattled off another few "someone calleds"—a list that was, among other things, notable for its lack of diversity. And then he rattled off about two dozen names, each followed by a head shake from me. "Nope, nope, nope, nope, nope, nope, nope..." Not only had I not read them, I had never heard of most of them. When I had, I would shout like some kind of game show contestant, "Yes! Yes! I know that one!"

"So," he said, not a trace of judgment in his voice. "It looks like you have some catching up to do."

The truth is, all these years later, I still have a lot of catching up to do. For a woman in my profession, I am woefully poorly read. It has been impossible, while raising three kids and launching a brand new career, to make up for nearly fifteen years of unexercised literacy. And strangely enough, because this mid-life attempt to have a writing career has led to book publication, I now have even less time for reading the masterworks of those missing years. Many weeks all I read are student stories, books I might blurb, contest entries, manuscripts by friends who need feedback, and also new books out by writers I know—or new books by writers I admire. I read a lot, but ask me about any famous, critically-acclaimed book written in the late eighties or the nineties, and the odds are overwhelmingly good that I haven't read it.

I have long been ashamed of this fact. I try not to be, but so far no success. And there are outside influences that make it hard. Any number of very vocal reading devotees, prominent in my corner of social media, seem to look down on those who don't read much; or haven't read much lately; or have had to set that pleasure aside for other demands—or even for other pleasures more suited to that period of their lives. It is hard to still carry the deficits of a non-reader and not feel the sting of that scorn.

I'm hardly an advocate for illiteracy. I want everyone to read and read a lot. I want everyone to find the exquisite pleasure I experienced just this morning, snow outside, a fire lit, a transporting novel on my lap. But I also want people to consider not saying things like, "I don't understand people who don't read"—in tones that suggest this is a failing of some kind, as if their own reading renders them somehow superior—as opposed to privileged. Because although, yes, sometimes not reading is a sign of an incurious nature or a lazy imagination, it can also be a sign of a too stressful life. Or of emotional pain. Or a learning disability. Or economic realities. Or of many, many other things, none of which indicate flaws in character.

Though maybe in my case it was a character flaw that averted my gaze from the written word. Maybe I was cowardly in keeping my distance from a world that made me regret my path. Maybe I let my envy rule the day, and opted for self-protection over full engagement. Maybe my excuses still ring a little hollow to me because there was an element of choice involved.

A friend wrote me recently that it is good to have the pressure of unfinished business in one's life. Yes, I suppose that it is—and for me, some of that pressure takes the form of too many spines uncracked, pages unread, characters unmet, stories unknown—and of a shame that may well stay with me all my days, deserved or not.

Rejection, Summer Conference Style

EVERY SUMMER, A FEW people I know will mention that they'll be departing soon for the Sewanee Writers Conference. I hear that it's amazing. I believe that it must be. For many years, I have observed the literary friendships it has inspired, the joys of insights gained, the happily drunken memories shared.

I applied there myself, in the early 2000s, twice. This was before I had any publications, and I was applying as a paying customer, not requesting anything other than admission, for which I would have been thrilled to cough up a healthy sum. Both years, however, I was placed on a waitlist from which I was then never plucked.

Fair enough. They either didn't much like my work, or didn't like my application essay—as I recall, there was one—or didn't cotton to my recommenders, if those were required, none of whom would have been well-known writers, since I knew none at the time. Any of that is reasonable. Rejection is part of the game. Or rather, rejection is part of the profession—a profession that can feel like a game.

But here is the dumbass part: I have never applied to another writing conference since. I have never applied as a paying customer, and I have made excuses not to apply even when nominated for a fellowship. "It's not a good summer to leave the family," I have said. Or, "I should spend any time I'm away working on my book."

Those excuses were, if not flat-out lies, at least hemi-demi-semi lies. I could have gotten around any of the above had I set my mind to the task. But I was afraid to apply. Even though I have long had a horrible case of Conference Envy. (Those friendships forged! Those insights gained! The parties! The fun!) But no. I have never even tried.

The easy explanation is that, having been demolished by those earlier rejections, I suffer from a minor, comedic version of PTSD. Oh, did I not mention that I was demolished? The weeping that ensued? The resultant certainty that no ambition I held dear would be fulfilled? The self-loathing? The even longer than usual suffering of my long-suffering husband who withstood the onslaught of my misery with stoic, unconditional love? Even when I yelled at him for trying to reassure me. (Hint to partners of writers who are in self-hating devastation mode: Don't try to reassure them. Just weather the storm and maybe bake brownies or restock the liquor cabinet, depending on the vice of choice. Or step away and save yourself.)

Meanwhile, in the ensuing years, while avoiding ever letting a conference reject me again ("As God is my witness…I will never…") I have, of course, put myself up for and received all manner of other rejections. Stories are sent back with perfunctory comments scrawled. Essays are turned down, without a word. Editors are "underwhelmed" by a book. Prizes are allocated elsewhere; grant applications, refused. All in the course of a day's work, or perhaps a life's work. You put yourself out there, you take your lumps. You do it again. You do it. I do it. Again and again and again.

Except when it comes to conferences. No way, no how. Not me.

So why the difference? I think there's an obvious answer—and then, I think there may be another answer, too. The first, the most logical, is that those tolerable if unpleasant rejections listed above are very clearly rejections of my *work*. They mean that I won't see a piece of mine in print, or won't have the pleasure of reading my name on a list, or won't receive money of which I believe I'd make good use.

But they do not mean that people don't want to spend ten days with me. They aren't rejections of my company, not rejections likely to reverberate with memories of social exclusion, with lifelong fears of being disliked. Being the weird kid at school who wasn't invited to the cool kid birthday parties. And, though the Sewanee rejections were no doubt also rejections of my work, at the time they felt like rejections of *me*.

We're having a gathering, and we don't want you there.

Ouch.

So I have preemptively exiled myself, perhaps to real loss. As the saying goes, nothing ventured, nothing gained. And of course this leads to a lesson, a simple lesson for one and for all: *Don't let yourself take any rejection so personally that it limits your attempts to participate fully in your profession. Just don't.*

Makes sense to me.

And I could stop here, I know, and call this a thoroughly digested experience. But, as I said, there is a second possible way to view this avoidance of mine: Perhaps I exercised a kind of twisted, inadvertent wisdom by scapegoating those Sewanee rejections, casting them as *just beyond* the limit of what I could tolerate.

Suppose I had never applied to Sewanee. Suppose my only experiences of rejection were of the kind I describe above, the ones that, while painful, don't have the same devastating impact on me. Would I really have gone through this career setting no limits on my ability to make myself vulnerable? Would there truly have been no category of intolerable rejection from which I needed to protect myself, no pain so bad that I would refuse to endure it again?

I wonder. It's entirely plausible that I designated a variety of vulnerability as intolerable—in order to tolerate any vulnerability at all. And summer conferences. I mean, yes, they sound pretty damn good from where I'm sitting, never having been to one. But they aren't necessary to a career. They aren't in the same category as submitting to magazines, querying agents. They aren't the defining risks of a writer's career without which there is no career. So perhaps I was smart to corral so much of my anxiety, telling myself that no matter what happened, whatever other rejections I faced, I would never have to go through *that* again.

I surely needed coping mechanisms. Stepping into the world with what felt to me like the outpourings of my most private secret self was unimaginably difficult. I had kept myself more or less limited to a life inside my home for two decades, for many reasons—including a shattering anxiety about rejections of all sorts, a certainty that I would fail at anything I tried, and a conviction that failing would then push me right back home.

But somehow, though I have had my share of failures along the way, I have withstood them and pushed on, often to my own surprise.

Regret is a funny thing. On one level, I do regret the many summers when I have stayed out of the competition, and therefore, maybe, also out of an important aspect of "the game." But the problem with that particular regret is that while playing it safe in that way, I managed to emerge from the tiny private world in which I kept myself. I managed to put together a career as a writer. I weathered a lot of disappointment without being demolished, or retreating from the larger goal. And so I wonder if this small, arguably symbolic act of self-protection wasn't a necessary concession to the anxious, fearful part of myself.

And so, some alternate advice: *Do whatever you have to do, avoid whatever you need to avoid, protect yourself however you need to protect yourself in order to stay on course, write, send the work out, write more, send out more work. Because as wonderful as the rest of it may be, conferences, Twitter, writing groups, and so on, if they are more than you can handle, that's okay. But if you stop writing and stop sending your work into the world, that is not okay. That is giving up.*

In my heart of hearts, I believe this is the real message.

Meanwhile, another summer has gone by. I am facing any number of potential rejections and disappointments. Who knows how my next book will be received? Or the next story I write? The range of possibility is mind-boggling. But at least I have once again protected myself—perhaps neurotically, perhaps wisely—from that one intolerable vulnerability. A bit wistful about what I have possibly precluded, but only a bit, both the envy and the relief just more rituals of my writing life, by now.

The Dreaded Desk Drawer Novel

IN AN IDEAL WORLD, if you start your career a couple of decades after you'd hoped, whatever urgency you feel will result in productive efficiency. For me, that has *sometimes* been the case. But there is a fine line between constructive urgency and the kind of panic that is anything but useful—a line that unfortunately I have crossed.

When I started writing my first novel, I was forty-two, working on short stories at the same time, including those in my collection. The stories were endlessly exciting to me, little puzzles with which I became obsessed, and I loved writing them, even though for every one I finished, I abandoned more than I can recall.

That part could be disheartening, but I began to recognize it as my work style—many projects happening at once, a lot of pages never making it off my hard drive. I was a writer who needed to play with ideas in order to learn skills, and in order to find the words containing heat. And though the pace frustrated me—after all, I was "older" with no sign of book publication yet—I also accepted the process, in large part because, with each finished story, I felt a sense of accomplishment. And I could publish stories individually, so even without a book, and even as I discarded close to eighty percent of the short fiction I wrote, I received the thrill that publication brings.

•

At the same time, I began hanging out with writers more and more, some through my MFA program, others in Philadelphia, where I live, and I started hearing a lot about the "desk drawer novel." It seemed like a phenomenon people took for granted. "And then, of course, there's my starter novel. *That* thing will never see the light of day."

Their casual tone flipped me out. My confident stance: *I do not have time for that.*

After all, these writers were talking about novels they had written in their twenties! Maybe their early thirties! It was one thing for me to toss out failed stories, but to put years into a full-length book and then abandon it? At that rate I'd be in my fifties before I published a novel! There was just no way. I had started one, I was progressing with it, and it was The Novel. It had to be.

So great was my determination that I actively ignored clear signs that there were problems with The Novel even as I steadily added more and more pages. I never questioned why I wouldn't show it to the friends who normally read my works in progress, not even my mother, whom I trust with just about everything I write. And I didn't pause to probe why every time I opened The Novel on my screen I felt a kind of detachment, a sense of confusion over why this novel was my novel, what it had to do with me. I had always understood why I wrote the stories I wrote. The themes resonated for me, the plots fascinated me. I couldn't wait to share them with readers—and none of that was true of this longer work. Yet the word count went up, the scenes accumulated. I labored on, barely letting myself know what I knew—a bit like a married person who can feel the union crumbling and is frantically staying busy to avoid the truth.

I even went so far as to sell it as part of a two-book deal, when I was about three years into the project. I didn't sell it on the basis of the many pages I had (which I still wouldn't show anyone, even my agent) just the first fifty, and a summary of the rest. There was nothing cynical or duplicitous about the sale. It would be fine, I told myself, convincingly enough. The story collection would come out first and by then, the novel would have survived its awkward adolescence and somehow blossomed into a book of which I could be proud.

But things don't always go as one plans, much less as one hopes. My editor didn't want to publish the stories first. She wanted me to take a few months to whip the novel into shape so we could move forward. And on one level that was thrilling. I was just shy of forty-seven when I sent in the draft, so I could still get that novel out in the world before I turned fifty—the arbitrary goal I had set.

That fall and winter I worked and worked and worked, feeling increasingly as though I were working on some random manuscript that kept inexplicably materializing on my computer screen. The situation, the location, the people all felt alien and uninteresting. But maybe that was just fatigue, I told myself. Maybe working on anything for so long leads to inevitable boredom. No writer has perspective on her own work, I reminded myself. So I pushed through my doubts, got it into the best shape I could, tried to believe that I was being too hard on myself, and hit send.

And then I waited. And waited.

The day of reckoning came several weeks later when I was called to New York to meet with my editor and her assistant. The vibe in the room was not good, my capacity to rationalize, ebbing fast. Nobody said anything harsh but nobody said anything enthusiastic either, and as the other women in the room went through the copious changes they thought should be made, discussing their responses to the characters, I felt very little beyond the desire to say, *I know this isn't my best work, I'm so sorry that I wasted everybody's time*, and cut the meeting short.

I didn't, but I must have conveyed something of what I felt, because my editor never handed me her notes, though they were extensive, and she had initially said that she would. Shortly after that meeting, she decided to publish the story collection first.

Even then, I didn't give up. As difficult as this is for me now to believe, I was so horrified at the thought of having wasted more than four years on a "starter novel," that I simply couldn't bear the thought of starting again. And so for another six months, I dug away at the thing, changing the point of view, changing the tense, removing one character, putting in another, aware of two things as I did: First, that these are common revision practices and don't by themselves mean a manuscript is doomed. And second, that this particular manuscript was doomed.

I pronounced it officially dead a few months before my story collection came out. The timing wasn't a coincidence. Imminent publication was the nail in the coffin of my denial. While I knew the stories might find detractors, as all books do, I also knew I could stand behind them as my best work. But no amount of effort would make this novel into something I wanted out in the world. Possibly, it could be patched together into an okay book, but never into one of which I would be proud. My editor was gracious—perhaps relieved—and sent me off with the mandate that I try again, and write the best novel I could write.

I used this as an excuse to replace my old computer, and I have never looked at those files again.

My awareness of my age plays many roles in this story, some conflicting. I stuck with the first novel longer than made sense, because I couldn't bear to have "wasted" years, to postpone the dream any longer, a set of emotions that fueled some impressive denial. But of course, ignoring my gut feeling that the book warranted abandonment only led to my wasting more years.

It's easy to be irritated with myself, but this is a terribly challenging balance to strike for those of us who feel the pressures of time. It is hard enough to judge one's own work under any circumstance, and harder still when a kind of panic distorts your view. How do you respond to that urgency productively, savoring the days and making the most of the months, while not letting awareness of age, even mortality, morph into the sort of anxiety that warps your judgment?

I'm not sure there is a single answer, but I know where I took my wrong turn.

C.S. Lewis writes, in a very different context: "If you look for truth, you may find comfort in the end; if you look for comfort you will not get either comfort or truth, only soft soap and wishful thinking to begin, and in the end, despair."

Well, maybe not exactly despair in this case. After all, I am talking about a modest professional setback, and not the religious struggles of a lifetime, as Lewis was. But for sure my privileging a comforting fiction over a truth I pretended not to know cost me years that might have been far better spent, ones that I could ill afford to lose.

Because, in the end, of course, it wasn't the story on the page that tripped me up. It was the story that I told myself.

My Parent Trap

THERE ISN'T MUCH ABOUT parenting that I don't know. Mothering, specifically. An important caveat though: I mean, mothering with a good dose of privilege, including, critically, financial security. But within that fortunate realm, I have been at this mothering thing for more than half my life. I have been a happily married mom, an unhappily married mom, a single mom, a blended family mom, a stay-at-home mom, a working mom. I have a child with special needs. I have children who are academic superstars—and have their own challenges, nonetheless. Children who have been through depressions. Children who have periods of being angry at me. Children who have had trouble separating from me. I have straight children. I have a gay child. I had a married child—and now I have a divorced one.

Write what you know, they say. Mothering is what I know. It's where the bulk of my experience lies. And I love being a mother. I'm one of those mothers who touches base with her grown kids nearly every day, who counts them among her closest friends. I send treacle-sweet texts with hearts and baby animal emoticons. I end each phone call with a giant "MWAH!"—and so do they. It's all a little revoltingly cute…And yet…

When my story collection came out, a collection very much about relationships between parents and children, I was often asked—in carefully worded terms—why a notable number of the mothers in the book were so…whatever the opposite of warm and fuzzy is. So severe. So unsentimental about their children. Where was the gushing? The snuggling? Where the adoration? The idealization?

It was a funny set of questions, but a fair one. Funny, because the kind of mother missing from the bulk of my stories is in many ways the kind I have been, the kind I am. And my own mother, while not sugary sweet, is anything but cold. So whence these rather severe women I had created, all viewing their offspring with a decidedly jaundiced eye? I wasn't really sure.

After the stories, when I started to try (and try, and try) to write a novel to replace the one I had abandoned, all of my attempts were again heavy on parent/child themes. That wasn't a conscious decision, but an unexamined continuation of the assumption that I should write what I know. I was aware, as I began each failed attempt, that the mothers in these pieces were again unsentimental to the point of being acerbic. Their relationships with their children were uniformly cool, bordering on frosty. They saw flaws far more easily than they perceived any characteristics you might term lovable. And I saw that these forays were only that: forays. None made it much past fifty pages, though a few did make it that far. But then I grew bored, and the projects died, one by one, one and all.

Many elements contributed to my sudden undying attachment to the novel I ended up writing, but a vivid aspect was my decision to make my central couple childless. Not only that, I made my narrator, a woman, motherless as well. I took the subject of maternity out of the center of the work.

A confession: I love being a parent, but I do not find the subject of parenting particularly interesting. I have learned this about myself by reading my own fiction—and by producing it. In spite of having written so much about mothering, I'm not notably keen on parent/child relationships in stories or novels—especially when it comes to young children. Friendship has led me to read some stellar novels primarily on the subject, but going by jacket copy alone, I would be unlikely ever to pick one up.

(I'm tempted here to offer explanations for my preferences, but doing so would imply that this particular preference requires a defense beyond the fact that some of us are interested in some things, others of us in others. And it shouldn't need such a defense, and so I won't.)

I didn't know that motherhood wasn't particularly *my thing*, fictionally speaking, during the eight years when I wrote my story collection. Maybe, with my children still so young, my footing in the writing world unsteady at best, I couldn't let myself know that. Maybe my brain was so filled with those concerns that I couldn't imagine beyond them. The subject seemed to belong to me. My evolving theory is that these cold mothers of mine were a kind of grudging, unconscious compromise between the fact of motherhood being my primary area of expertise for all my adult years, and my own intellectual neutrality on the subject. It seems possible, even likely, that those chilly women are the embodiments of my ambivalence not about mothering but about my assumption that I had been elected by fate to write about it—a lot. I imagine them now, these severe moms, as stand-ins for my saying outright, "I may have been a stay-at-home mother for all my adult life, but please do not assume that means I'm some kind of baby-crazy, sentimental nurture machine, endlessly fascinated by the subject of the mother-child bond. Because I'm not."

But that's just me. Well, it's me and the many (many!) aspiring writers I know who have told me some version of: "I know I'm supposed to write what I know, but I've been a housewife for twenty years. And no one wants to hear about that. *I* don't even want to hear about that…"

Or actually this isn't even about just me and them. Full-time stay-at-home parents can't be the only people who find a disconnect between the life they have led, through choice or fear or who-knows-what, and their creative, intellectual concerns. (Nor do all stay-at-home parents find the subject distant from their creative selves, as I now do. It is not, after all, an inherently uninteresting subject.)

Perhaps, though, it's no coincidence that being a stay-at-home mother led to a timidity of imagination in me, one against which I still fight. We "full-time" mothers are not culturally encouraged to be bold or adventurous in matters intellectual. I have only to conjure the indulgent condescension of acquaintances, when I first admitted to "wanting to write," in order to remember just how discouraged I was to do so—much less to write about anything outside the realm of child-rearing. (A shocking number assumed I meant children's books.) Some of that has changed, I think, I hope, with the internet, with greater communication from home to home, from home to outside world, but when I was in the thick of it, endless antiquated messages about what it meant about one's intellectual capacities to be home with the kids still came through, unmistakably demeaning.

To the extent that the advice to "write what you know" honors a writer's history, though that history may be different from what is traditionally deemed "literary," the advice is doubtless affirming. But "write what you know" can also be a limiting mandate that assumes that you are artistically shackled to your life as lived. And that is bad—for many reasons, including that authenticity of experience is by no means the only kind of authenticity that produces the best work. Authenticity of passion is at least as mighty an engine, I would think.

When I was writing my novel, on the inevitable low days, when I had lost the thread—not of the plot, but of the project—I would fall back on the old advice, "Write the book that is missing from your shelf, the one that you wish you could read." That gave me the inspiration I needed. Not because it reminded me of what I know, but because it reminded me of why I write, why I care about this process at all, why it's important to me. It reminded me that reading saved my life when I was an unhappy child, of how liberating storytelling can be *particularly* from the facts of one's own existence, how mysterious, how beautiful, how incomprehensible that power, how impossible to understand. How very important a role is played by the unknown in any act of imagination. The book I most wanted to read was a book that could teach me more than I could teach it.

Does this mean that the next novel I write will be about people who have absolutely nothing in common with me? Will it require decades of research? Flights of fancy the likes of which I've never taken in the past?

I have no idea. And that's the point. But from now on, when I write a mother who is a little severe on the subject of her children, a little tough, I'll be doing it on purpose, and not unknowingly voicing a complaint about my own unexamined misunderstanding of the art I am allowed to make.

AD(H)D II: August 8, 2011

TO DO[12]
Work Stuff:[3]
Novel, novel, novel[4]
Finish PH blurb[5]

---

1   August 8, 2011, originally handwritten.

2   For as long as I can remember I have made TO DO lists with the letters all caps. Generally, they are handwritten and I get very compulsive about certain formatting things. The TO DO itself has to be bold—so I go over it many times—and the letters have to be exactly the same size with the T very close to the first O so it almost looks like one word but isn't quite. I sometimes think of the lists as TODO lists—pronounced pretty much like Dorothy's dog. It can take me several pieces of paper to get the formatting just right.

3   I always put Work Stuff first. That is an entirely meaningless fact.

4   The repetition of the word *novel* here is because it's really more of a cheer than a statement of fact. *Novel, novel, novel. You can do it, you can do it! Gooooo novel!* The one thing it doesn't mean is that I'll work on my novel.

5   This is my fourth or fifth blurbing experience. I've just started to realize how bloody difficult it is, even when you like a book a lot, to find things to say that don't sound like you bought them at the blurb store. Nobody gets to be fearless, heartbreaking, or insightful anymore. Nor can anything happen time and again. No sentences can begin with the word "with" as in: "With rare insight, this fearless author will break your heart time and again." That shit is over. But it doesn't leave me

Talk to H.[6]
Put stuff on calendar[7]
House:[8][9]
   1. Call about cushions[10]
   2. Paint DR chairs[11]

---

with an easy path.

6   H. is Henry, my agent. We don't have any business to discuss, but we've become good friends and it's been a while. Mostly, we talk about our kids. This shouldn't really be listed under "Work."

7   It has only just occurred to me, at the age of 49, that by writing things on a calendar, one increases the chance of doing them.

8   This spring, we considered moving out of our house in the 'burbs and into Center City, Philadelphia. But then (after seeing the prices in the city) we realized that it makes a lot more sense to stay here until our youngest is out of high school (three more years) but that as we're staying here, we had better spruce the place up a bit. This has become a huge, huge project. It is eating up our lives. But not in a bad way.

9   In the handwritten version, there is a little drawing of a house to the left of this word.

10   I made the mistake of ordering cushions from Calico Corner. They charge the earth which in a decent, fair world would mean they do a good job. But in fact they did it wrong and I have to take them back. I have written "Call about cushions" here but what I really need to do is drive out to Calico Corner and return the cushions. I just really don't want to do that. "Call about cushions," translated, really means: "Shit. I cannot believe I have to drive the effing cushions all the way out to Devon just because THEY did a crummy job. Maybe if I put it off, Richard will do it with me on Saturday."

11   I have a bad history with these chairs. Ten years ago, I started to re-cover them, then midway through the fourth chair—of six—decided I hated what I was doing. So there they have been, semi-covered ever since. Now, I have decided to paint them in that shabby chic, distressed kind of way. But I finished two chairs about a month ago and haven't started the others yet. People in this house are not

3. Kitchen!!!!!!!!!![12]
4. Living room?[13]
Dinner: Chicken—buy salad?[14]
Ask Richie about bike ride?[15]
Call optometrist for D.[16]
Call for haircut[17]

---

optimistic.

12   The exclamation marks are a howl of anguish. The kitchen is a disaster area and the odds of my cleaning it are low. Maybe the exclamation marks are a cry for help. Kitchen help.

13   Again, the punctuation here means as much as the words themselves. We have lived in this house for 16 years and I have never known how to decorate our living room. It's a funny shape. We don't really use it—we hang out in the kitchen. And it is now infested with moths—they lived in our couch (which has been in our driveway for a month now) and on the wool rug (which has been de-mothed and moved to a less conspicuous spot). So, this particular list item is a little miscategorized on a **TODO** list as I don't really mean to do anything. And I don't really need a reminder to wonder what the hell to do with the living room. But there it is.

14   I won't buy salad. It says "buy salad?" because we are trying to eat healthily and I want to think I will buy salad. But I won't.

15   We are also trying to exercise more. But the odds that my husband and I will go for a bike ride at 6:30 when he gets home are negligible. We never have, though this is a frequent feature of my **TODO** lists. Again, this entry is there mostly to make me feel like I am a better person than I am.

16   My son needs to have his eyes examined. This will actually get done.

17   This one will probably not get done. I have a lot of difficulty committing to haircuts. I usually have the idea of getting a haircut on the list in some form or other for at least two months before any appointment-making takes place.

Meds[18][19]

---

18   There are some prescriptions that need to be refilled—for my ADD. In theory they help me do things like execute the tasks on my **TODO** lists.

19   Hmmmmm...

The Art of Ripping Stitches

LINGERING ON VARIOUS HARD drives in my possession right now are the abandoned beginnings to at least two hundred short stories. Some are mere opening lines, but several dozen stretch as long as fifteen pages or more. Twenty or thirty are fully drafted; I have just never been able to revise them to my own satisfaction. I may go back to one or two over time, but probably not. In other words, for every one of the eleven stories in my first book I have started approximately twenty more.

Which means that every time I begin a story, I do so in the knowledge that the odds are pretty slim that I'll ever finish it, that the overwhelming likelihood is that I will work on it for days, even weeks, sometimes years, and then lose faith.

I also have several dozen similarly abandoned essays, three novels that made it past the fifty page mark, and the big one, the 300-page novel that I worked on for four years and revised at least three times. May it rest in peace.

I'm not sharing these gruesome statistics because I think I'm a special case, but because I think it's not all that far from the norm. We are all struggling here. We are all making false starts, falling in and out of love with our own words, facing hard truths about something we have labored on for what seems like an eternity. And we are all haunted by the belief that it's a whole lot easier for everyone else.

A couple of years ago, at a post-reading dinner, a well-known writer and I got to talking about how impossible it is to predict which of one's students will keep writing over time. I suggested that maybe success—defined as continuing to write—is determined by three things: talent, hard work, and good luck, and that without some of all three, it's very hard to keep going. My dinner companion added another.

"You have to be good at being a writer," he said. "You have to be able to survive it all."

The conversation moved on, and I can't remember if I ever asked him exactly what he meant, but I know what *being good at being a writer* means to me. Most obviously, it means being able to keep going in spite of the inevitable rejection from others. But perhaps more critically it means being able to survive rejection from oneself, to weather the huge number of failed attempts and dashed hopes, the daily sense that one is not actually good enough to do what one wants so desperately to do. It means being able to wake up many mornings having disappointed oneself the day before and once again resuscitate the capacity to hope that this day's result will be different. And it means learning to recognize that every word one writes is just as important as every other word, that the words that make it out into the world cannot exist without those that came before, now lingering on a hard drive, abandoned.

Process, process, process, process.

One of the wisest things ever said to me about writing was said to me about sewing. Years ago, when I wanted to make my own clothing, an older woman told me, "If you're going learn how to sew, you're going to have to learn to love ripping out stitches. Otherwise, you'll quit."

I stopped sewing a quarter century ago, but I have never stopped reminding myself of that.

On Learning to Spell Women's Names
While Men Buy My Novel
for Their Wives

I WAS AT A party, a celebration of my novel, thrown by old friends, and filled with couples around my age, middle-aged men and women. My host asked me to read a bit from the book, which I did, and I answered some questions about my process and about the publishing world; and then I stepped out of the spotlight so that something closer to a normal party might begin. A normal party that included one guest selling and signing books, that is.

Such interactions are inherently a little awkward. I felt both fortunate and a bit sheepish, as I always do when making chit-chat while selling my wares. But this time I also felt a different, distinct discomfort settling in as more than one man approached me, book in hand, and told me he wanted to buy it—as a present for his wife. *You can make it out to...Carol...Jane...Kathy...*

I began to feel grumpy. I don't believe it showed, but I was starting to feel unmistakably irked at the unspoken assumption that I had written a book for women. Only women. That a man who bought a copy for himself might as well also buy a pair of heels and some jewelry to accessorize the purchase.

To be clear, I wasn't ticked off at these individual men. They were—to a man, so to speak—warm and encouraging, said kind things about the work I'd read aloud, and expressed interest in the whole process of how a book comes into the world. My friends are lovely people, and they had gathered lovely friends of their own. But…One particularly engaging man told me he belonged to a book group. A men's book group. "You should suggest this to them," I said, poking a bit, consciously making mischief.

At least he was forthcoming. "It's really tough to get them to read books written by women," he said. "It's viewed as…" He shook his head and shrugged.

Sigh.

I'm not describing an unfamiliar phenomenon here. The fact that it's difficult to get men to read fiction by women has been well-documented and mightily discussed. But something about this experience, the line of actual, living, breathing men armed with spellings of women's names, made the imbalance feel *true* and—excuse me—*just so fucking weird,* in a way that no statistics, no documented trends ever have.

Really, guys? Really?

Yes. Really.

It never occurs to me when I write that I am writing for one sex almost exclusively. To me, I am just a person, writing fiction for other people to read. I am concerned with the simple, central question of why people do what they do. Is that a particularly feminine preoccupation? I hope not. I hope it's something we're all thinking about, a lot.

"Men love this book," I finally said to one fellow guest, thinking of the men who have, most of them friends and family, their ages ranging from 23 to 81. "You might be surprised."

"Well, I did like what you read, a lot…"

Dot. Dot. Dot. Awkward silence.

All righty, then. I guess I'm not going to change the world at a book party.

"And how is Carol spelled? Is there an e?"

I'm not angry at any individual. I'm not a bit sure I'm angry at all, though the word is, of course, inevitably, tiresomely melded to all observations that might be termed "feminist"—and so I feel some obligation to contend with the presumption. In truth, a bit weary, on this day anyway, I feel more frustrated than angry.

And the frustration is familiar, like some kind of natural element, innate to existence by now. It disperses into the air we all breathe and refills my lungs; strolls with me down sidewalks; prickles, uncomfortable, as I watch stereotypes play out on my TV. This is not only the fault of those men who bought my book. This a Big Social Problem, and so society, culture, history must all shoulder the blame—though, of course, as always, it falls on individuals to fix what entire civilizations have broken. It isn't ever acceptable to let the weariness win out.

Or, it turns out, to forget to be angry. Or to disown the emotion because others have used its name as a weapon against women… Shame on me for that. Anger it is.

And so the analysis begins anew: *Why don't men read books by women?*

Friends and I have puzzled over this endlessly. Is it the fear of being seen holding a pink cover, a logical if unfortunate response to an unabashedly traditional gender-coded message that literary marketing has sent? Is it the outgrowth of a process that begins with people telling newborn girls how sweet and pretty they are, encouraging them as they grow, to be nice and worry about relationships, while telling boys how big and strong they are, encouraging them to be tough and smart? Does that well-documented distinction make reading what women write—always presumptively about domestic relationships—seem a feminine activity? (While not making reading male authored fiction about domestic relationships problematic—as if those books have some kind of *blue-for-boys, won't-lessen–your-manhood* stamp of approval on them.) Is this just another corner of the world in which those who are taught to view women as equated with emotions, and emotions as equated with weakness (and therefore, by the transitive property…) reward the lifelong brainwashing inflicted on them by acting accordingly?

Do girl books have girl cooties? Is it really that much a legacy of the schoolyard? Of the nursery?

Probably. That's all doubtless part of it. But, having gone through what felt like a strangely ritualistic enactment of a statistic I haven't wanted to believe, I am filled more with questions about the larger *implications* of men not reading fiction by women than about the causes.

If you think that because I'm female what I have to say in my novel won't interest you, what about the things I say when I am talking to you about the research project in which we're both engaged? About the funding needed for the public school system? How about when I am arguing a case in court? Filing an insurance claim?

Is it credible that fiction occupies a unique place? Credible that men who dismiss what female storytellers have to say as irrelevant to them aren't also inclined to dismiss—perhaps unconsciously—what females of every variety have to say? To think it somehow less relevant than what men say? Is it credible that this literary aversion is a special case of some kind? A glitch?

Just as the fact that men commonly skip over female authors has never felt as real to me as it now does, the implications of that fact have never seemed as serious. And though I am limiting my exploration here to "men" and "women" as if our genders divide anything like so clearly, I have no doubt that these issues are all the more complex and disheartening for those whose gender does not fit mainstream definition.

But back to the mainstream for a moment, back to traditional gender presumptions, which are almost certainly at the root of all this. The book that I wrote has been described in reviews as *tense, taut*, and *brutal*. I'm not suggesting that had it been called *tender, sweet*, and *heart-warming*, men would be right not to read it, but when you write a book so commonly described with adjectives that are viewed in this (dysfunctional, sexist) society as "male," and men *still* aren't interested in reading it because the author is female, it's …it's depressing. That's the word. Depressing. And enraging.

I am bummed out about this. Not because I don't value my female readers nor because of the impact on my career or sales numbers, but because of the questions to which this imbalance inevitably leads, because of my hunch that this book-avoiding nonsense is only a relatively innocuous hint at something much more important, something both endemic and profoundly ugly, something that has precious little to do with literary taste.

In Which My Mother Suggests
That I Murder Her,
As a Marketing Ploy

ON THE PHONE WITH my beloved mother, I was—once again—bemoaning the difficulties of getting attention for my quiet, literary novel. "It's a good book," I said. "I honestly believe that. And I feel like if I could just get more people to know about it…I have completely lost faith in all social media crap, and I just keep wondering if there's some kind of scandal I could get involved in that might help."

"Not a terrible idea," my mother said. (I love my mother.)

We talked then for a while about the possibilities. I ruled out a sex scandal, based on loving my husband and thinking that having already asked him to put up with a lot for my writing career, that might just be a bridge too far. "I could maybe find some way to make it look like I plagiarized the whole thing. Plagiarized books get a lot of attention. People get famous for that shit."

"But don't the publishers sometimes destroy all copies?"

"I suppose. Though that might still help with the next book. I could commit a crime. Except I don't fancy time in prison."

"You could kill someone," my eighty-one-year-old mother said.

"I suppose."

"You could kill me," she said. "I'm old."

I have to tell you, I was really touched. "How would I get away with it?" I asked. "Or should I even get away with it? I mean, is it enough just having my mother killed, or do I kind of need, for full publicity and all, to be accused of doing it?"

"Ideally," she said, "from a publicity perspective, I would think the best would be for you to be the prime suspect, but ultimately not convicted. Better for my grandchildren, too."

"Maybe I could claim insanity. Over wanting more attention for my book. A crime of passion. Because it is in fact making me insane."

"I don't think that works," she said.

"I could pin it on one of my brothers," I said, never too old to try to trick Mom into saying I'm her favorite.

"I can't go along with that," she said in her *that's not funny* voice.

"It was worth a shot."

"We'll figure something out," she said.

But soon enough, before we could work on the mechanics, she had to get off the phone. And I don't suppose we ever will come up with a plan for my killing her with which we're both entirely comfortable, probably not, but I really appreciate her willingness to go "all in" on this PR thing.

And of course, behind all the jokes and schemes lies a frustrating truth: There is essentially nothing an author can do to make her book break through the public consciousness, yet it is impossible not to try to figure out what the elusive, non-existent thing might be. Social media is a fantasy land when it comes to making sales. For my money, Twitter is spitting in the wind—though not from a social perspective; I have made good friends on there. But I would love to see a serious study of how effective Twitter is for selling books. I would be shocked to hear that it has much impact at all.

On Twitter and also Facebook, you are largely talking to people who already know about you and your work. Maybe if you are a best-seller and your publisher announces to their 300,000 followers that your next book is soon to launch, it has an impact. But when I tell the same 3,500 people anything over and over again, it has only an irritating effect.

The other thing authors are told to do is to "get their name out there" which translates into blogging (for free) and writing pieces for magazines and newspapers. But no author I know thinks that ever does more than shift a few books. Maybe, bit by bit, your name becomes known; but most of us would rather spend that same time writing our next book—and some of us feel pretty vehement about that. Recently, I told a classroom of students that if they spent precious writing time building a platform, I would personally chop it down. Nonsensical maybe, but I made my point.

The things that sell large numbers of books are entirely outside an author's control. Things like winning giant prizes. Things like being famous already. Things like having a household-name author make a mission of getting attention for your book. Or having Oprah hit you with what a friend calls "the happy stick." Movie deals sell books. Billboards in Times Square sell books. And all of these have in common that an author has zero zilch zippo control over any of it.

So what can an author do, short of murdering her mother, to seize the book buying public's attention? Despite the fact that I still spend sleepless hours gnawing at this question, convinced there must be a good answer, in fact, I believe there is only a bad one: nothing. An author has essentially no control over whether a book does or does not catch fire.

So the question is, now what? What do you do with being told that for some period of post-release, it's your job to market your book, if you believe that nothing you are positioned to do will cause the book to break though?

My own answer, now, after years of turning myself inside out, is to do only what I enjoy. I shut down my Facebook Author page because it brought me no pleasure and seemed mostly like a way of doubly annoying my Facebook friends. I tweet for fun and occasionally to publicize something and often to thank someone who has said something kind—or to say something kind about a colleague. But I don't approach it as though it's going to sell my books in any serious way—because it isn't. I write for magazines when the topic interests me and when the money is good. I blog because I happen to love blogging. I give readings because I like meeting readers, and because I so appreciate the booksellers who do what they can for authors of every kind. But with none of these activities do I ever let myself think: This is going to sell tons of books.

I think instead: These are the activities that being an author has given me access to, and I enjoy doing them, I am privileged to do them, and so I do. And in this way, I'm sure, I do sell some books along the way, but nothing like the numbers that send a novel into the stratosphere of which we all dream.

That is not an outcome I can force or woo or contrive. Or even influence. And doing so isn't my job. My job is to write. Thank god.

And my mother's job is to listen to me vent, and to encourage me to get back to the keyboard, which she does. Oh, and to be my very best reader, always, which is just one of an infinite number of reasons that this latest scheme of ours is no more than yet another marketing plan I will never try.

Shut Up, Shut Down

I HAD DINNER RECENTLY with a writer friend whose career is the envy of all, certainly the envy of me—one of those writers who by any standard is taking the world by storm. A critical success. A commercial success. Winner of prize after prize after prize. But he didn't have his mind on any of that. Rather, he was obsessing on the vitriol of some of his online anonymous reader reviews. And this wasn't a form of deflecting modesty—*let's not talk about my success, let's talk instead about the people who hated my book*—it was a genuine distress call, an appeal for help in managing the hurt he felt when he read these attacks—and let's be clear, that is the proper name for the ones that had upset him. They were not reviews in any but the loosest interpretation of that word.

"It makes me feel like never writing again."

I said the things one says. *You can't take it personally. It happens to absolutely every author. It's just noise. It reveals more about the person writing the so-called review than about the book.* These things are easy to say to someone else, less easy to hear in any particularly useful way when it's your turn to feel bruised by the bullying.

In the weeks since that conversation, and in the years since my own first book came out, I have thought a lot about this phenomenon of reader reviews that are not just negative, but vitriolic in a highly personal way. I have tried to understand what may underlie that vitriol and also why these bits of nastiness can be so genuinely hurtful when we all know how utterly meaningless they "ought" to be.

I'm not talking about people who are unmoved by a book, mine or anyone else's. I'm not talking about the person who says things along the lines of, *in the end, I felt the prose was weak* or *the characters left me cold.* I'm not even talking about the ones who say, *I really disliked this book from start to finish and am not sure why I read the whole thing.* I am—as was my friend—talking about the people who write things like, *I can't believe she thought I'd care about her stupid story,* or *I can just imagine him thinking he's so impressive by using all those long words,* or *so-and-so obviously has pretty bad relationships if he thinks people are like that.* In other words, the readers whose dislike of a book seems to lead to contempt—even hatred—for the author.

The first time it happened to me, I was stunned. Not at the fact of someone disliking my work, for which I was as prepared as one can be, but at the anger directed my way. I was stunned until I realized that the anger makes a kind of sense if one thinks of such a reader as being—in his own view—like any consumer who buys a product that doesn't "work." My "whiny" stories were no different from a toaster that blows a fuse because the construction is shoddy. I spew venom about companies with lousy workmanship. I question their decency in taking my money for something that didn't perform. And that is exactly how some readers react to the authors of books that didn't work for them.

Which should be reason to dismiss the whole thing with a shrug, maybe even a laugh. Yet I rarely see any writers laugh at the most vitriolic of their reviews.

Beyond the obvious fact that it's inherently unpleasant to have people call you nasty names, it's also likely that such personal invective feels *so* bad in part because its opposite, the love with which some readers so generously respond, feels *so* good. If we are to let ourselves believe all the praise, how do we not take in all the hatred? Live by the reader review; die by the reader review.

I also believe that most if not all writers share another quality that renders them particularly vulnerable to the charge that their work makes them despicable. So many writers felt silenced at a critical point in their lives. In some cases, such a taboo on truth-telling exists because of family secrets; in others it grows out of a secret kept about oneself; while in others the silencing force may be a political one, or have its roots in religion. But with pretty much every writer I know, some such taboo has been in place since childhood, sometimes since birth.

Of course, this is true of many people who aren't writers, too. Those people live with their own scars and their own challenges. But writers are a special case because the act of writing is itself a direct violation of taboos against speaking freely and honestly. The state in which many of us do our work is one of constant, internal battle between the silencing voices and the need to be heard over them. So the nastiest reviews, the most personal of them, the ones that demean our characters as they insult our work, are all too likely to find an echo, albeit an ancient one, within our hearts.

And this isn't just about nasty reviews. This has implications for any of us who write, whether reviewed or not. How much of what we call writers' block is in fact the result of our having internalized the message that if we fully express ourselves we are somehow "bad"? I often advise others (and remind myself) that the most efficient way to combat such blockage may not be to take such practical steps as being sure to sit at the keyboard every day, but to get angry at whatever internalized voices are encouraging you to stop writing, stop speaking up.

How often do we talk about writers who need "permission" when they are just starting out? How frequently do we see writers who inexplicably stop writing after they experience a level of success? After they experience the reality of speaking out and being heard?

In truth, it's all too easy to succumb to those silencing voices—whether they come from an anonymous reader or from forces we have been battling all our lives. It's all too easy for any of us to say, as my enviable friend did the other night, "It makes me feel like never writing again."

I speak from experience. Nearly twenty years of blank pages, fear and anxiety winning out. Taboos, winning out. I don't know why I was lucky enough, maybe stubborn enough, to triumph in that long-running argument with the echoing voices silencing me. I don't know that there are tricks I can share—beyond determination and outrage at the idea of being shut up, being shut down. But I do know that anyone who thinks that they should quit because they run the risk of being revealed as "bad," whether by readers or by ghosts, needs to put pen to paper, fingers to keyboard, and push on—because losing decades of your life to such fears leaves a very deep scar. And it turns out that even vicious responses to your work produce relatively superficial wounds—unless of course you allow them to do more.

Material

WHEN I FIRST MOVED to Philadelphia, in 1988, I had turned twenty-six a week before and given birth to my first child five weeks before that. My then husband (we have long since divorced) had a full-time job; while I had my infant daughter, a stroller, no friends, and a lot of hours on my hands every day. But it was spring, the best time of year to be out and about, so out and about I went.

Our home was located just two blocks away from Philadelphia's fabric district, Fourth Street, just below South Street, an area where twenty-seven years later I still shop for fabric when in need of curtains or new slipcovers, but that back in the late eighties seemed like it couldn't possibly last so long. It was then—as it still is now, as it has perhaps always been—a street spotted with businesses looking to be on their last legs, interspersed with vestiges of businesses already long gone.

It's an oddly bleak stretch, even in spring, even with bolts of colorful fabric spilling onto the sidewalk, but, bleakness and all, back in '88, it had a wonderfully welcoming feel, a vibe that hummed a familiar tune. I grew up with my grandmother living in our home, her six sisters frequent visitors. They were old school, their speech sprinkled with Yiddish, their stories often ones of the Lower East Side where their father had been a tailor in the early 1900s. The world of their memories was not the world of my own childhood—me, the daughter of university professors in Connecticut—but it took root, becoming something I carried inside myself, and still do. When I think about my grandmother's youth, the images I see, the atmosphere I feel, are all so vivid, they come to me much as memories of my own childhood do. The boundary between memory and imagination is a porous one.

Back in 1988, lonely, a little at sea with new motherhood, I passed hour after hour strolling those dreary blocks, admiring the fabrics, the silk tassels, the baskets of buttons, taking in the rhythms of the volleys between customers and salespeople, the bargaining and the near-physical heat that rose from a person tempted to buy something for more money than she should, the seduction of that. I loved the hints of Yiddish intonation to some voices—or maybe I just imagined them, as I imagined my own family, once upon a time, handling, measuring fabric on just such a street. There was so much about my life then that felt new—exciting in many ways, but also frightening. The sense I had of coming home, if only to a kind of ancestral home, soothed and strengthened me.

A quarter century later, some months into writing my novel *Life Drawing*, deep into the experiences of world creation and of trying to understand the people on my pages, I found myself with a central character, in Philadelphia, who had betrayed a beloved partner in the aftermath of losing a cherished sister. She felt isolated and scared. She felt like she had no home. It had been a very long time since my days of pushing a stroller on Fourth Street, but in wanting a "safe zone" for this woman who was facing a new, painful reality, I instinctively returned there. I invented a milliner shop, Steinman's, placed a brother and sister in charge—older, old school, with attitudes I remembered, attitudes I understood. I drew on a mix of my own memories and those I had inherited, long before. And I placed my character in the middle of the activity and the fabrics, where she sat painting a canvas and healing, for the course of a long bleak winter.

As different as her situation was from mine back when I found comfort amid the bolts of fabric, I understood, if only intuitively, that her needs were the same. And I understood too, as I hadn't in 1988, that even beyond matters of familiar accents and familial memories, there can be something oddly comforting about being among materials that are also in transition, yards of damask soon to be reinvented as drapes; buttons, loose and unattached, soon to be used to close a coat. There is comfort and there is *hope* in the knowledge that these unformed, not yet defined objects have such miraculous potential to be renewed.

For Augusta, my forlorn painter, watching the milliners craft marvels of beauty from bits and pieces of netting and velvet, scraps really, was just the healing experience she needed at the time. The promise of the unfinished, the inherent optimism of such transformation, all of it helped bolster her—as it had me when I was a new mother, lonely and scared.

Few days go by without someone asking me where I get my material. Puns aside, this tale of Fabric Row is typical—in part because I never had a single conscious thought, as I placed Augusta on Fourth Street, about why doing so felt so right. Material, for me, the fictional sort, is a matter of hunches and unexpected associations. I have only vague ideas, as I write, about why my stories take the turns they do, why they are set where they are, why my characters have the strengths and foibles that they have. And I like it that way.

But then I can almost always find evidence of an associative logic behind my choices, later on.

I still shop on Fourth Street when it's time for new slipcovers, or when a set of curtains has outlived its prime. Or sometimes when I just want to be in that place of optimism, and aspiration, and familiar cadences, once again. There is comfort for me, even now, on those eternally dreary blocks.

Father Chronicles:
To the Extent That He Was Able

"YOUR FATHER WOULD HAVE been so proud of you."

When my first book came out, more than one family friend told me this. Many tell me this still. For the most part, I only smile in response. Unless my mother is nearby, in which case, as soon as possible, I roll my eyes at her; and she nods her head, maybe shrugs her shoulders, in return.

That's about all the eloquence we need. We have reached the point at which gestures and code cover all we have to say, though the first time we heard mention of my father's hypothetical pride we talked it through.

"I don't think pride would be his primary response," I said in a cab back to her apartment from a gathering in New York. "I think he'd be absolutely flummoxed about how to respond to my having published a book."

"Unfortunately," she said, "I think you're right." And then we went on to remind each other of the many things we both already knew, but struggled with—and struggle with still, well over a decade after his death. His emotional instability, his crippling narcissism, his passionate longing for fame, the alcoholism that left him, even when sober, often preoccupied with longing for drink; and his lifelong desire to believe that he knew how to love.

"He really did love you kids," she said.

"To the extent that he was able," I said.

"To the extent that he was able," she said.

It is the mantra that hovers always in the overlap between my father's good intentions and the limitations that thwarted those, the same limitations that almost certainly played a role in thwarting my creative ambitions for so many years.

Causation and coincidence are not to be confused, but the fact that I was unable to write in any productive way until my father died, and then that I began to do so three weeks after his death, has always seemed more significant than any notions of mere coincidence would imply. That doesn't mean I fully understand what lies behind the timing, only that it's an important enough fact of my life that I cannot shake my sense that I should understand it. And so I look around for clues, particularly in the character of the man himself.

He wasn't modest, and like many immodest men, he didn't much like those who competed with him. His critiques of others in his professional field, notably those whose reputations rivaled or even overshadowed his own, were both scornful and condescending. This one was a "four-flusher," all flash, no substance. This other one was a second-rate mind. He had tags for those he deemed overrated and also for those he deemed pathetic in some way, worthy only of his pity, if worthy of notice at all. To compete with my father, it was clear, was to be despised or demeaned—or both.

Is it too simple to say that his paternity came laden with a similar non-compete clause? It's surely not something he knew about himself. I'm convinced that on every conscious level he wanted his children to succeed. But at the same time, he made it all too clear that anyone who tried to shine as bright as he became contemptible to him. And as for not shining as bright as he? Pitiable. Not worth the effort. These are the messages I internalized thoroughly enough that they stopped my fledgling ambitions in their tracks.

It can be liberating, yes, to recognize such a thing about one's own life, but it can also be deeply saddening to perceive the clarity of an unspoken conversation such as that, of mandates issued and followed, unaware. My father never imagining that through his actions he might be closing a child down. Me not comprehending how my behavior was shaped to appease this requirement of which he was unaware. I have no great certainty, looking back, about which of us to pity more.

And that is hardly the only thing about which I am unsure. My father's legacy is a profoundly unmooring one. In spite of all the troubles, I cannot dismiss him as a "bad" father nor, certainly, as a "bad" man. His desperation to be the most accomplished, most admired person in any room—if not the world—had about it the unmistakable quality of a psychiatric disorder, and to his credit he worked hard to battle his own instabilities. Moreover, his ambition was inextricably intertwined with a great deal of real good he did in the world, even as he made no bones about the motivating power of his hunger for fame. "For as long as I can remember, baby," he'd say in the Texas drawl that grew stronger with every decade he lived in the Northeast, "even as a boy, all I wanted was to be famous. There's never been any limit on that in me."

He never became a household name, but he was a massive figure in his field, legal academia, well-known for his work on civil rights, and through his writings in opposition to the death penalty. At Yale and Columbia Law Schools, where he taught for nearly a half-century combined, he educated scores of future leaders of every kind. When he died, his obituary ran a third of a page in the New York *Times*—a fact about which he himself would have been thrilled.

And it was impossible not be swept into his orbit. For much of my life, upon meeting people, I led with the fact of being his daughter. It seemed much more important an aspect of my identity than anything for which I might ever be responsible, and it also seemed somehow required of me.

To others it may have appeared as though I was bragging, mentioning this accomplished parent at every chance. But in fact, by mentioning him, I was keeping myself small, reminding myself how much more important he was than I, steadying myself through the gravity of his narrative, to which I was only appended, lightly attached.

"Your father would have been so proud of you."

I suppose it's inevitable that people say that, as it's inevitable that

I feel guilty about my certainty that it's incorrect. I have always felt guilty about perceiving his failings. "I haven't been a bad father, have I?" he asked, as he neared his death. "I've been all right, haven't I?"

The true answer was that he had indeed been a bad father, though he had not been only that. "Of course you've been all right, Dad. What are you even talking about?"

I had no desire to hurt him. Because I loved him, and because he loved me—to the extent that he was able.

And because complicated love produces complicated results. Having stifled my work for so long, he has also motivated it. An interviewer asked me recently whether I intend readers to dislike a particular character in my novel. My answer was that it's hard to exaggerate the degree to which I'm uninterested in trying to define whether my characters are good people or otherwise. I have long taken pride in not judging my own creations; and I understand now that this artistic point of view, this commitment to uncomfortable compassion, is a familiar vantage point for me, a place of primal security. For all that my father silenced me, he may also have given me one of the deepest, most cherished needs I possess: this hunger to comprehend the complexity of human behavior, to look beneath what might be dismissed as only hurtful, to discover what may neutralize simple dispositions of blame, to convey this to the world, if only to convince myself. In other words, to write.

You father would have been so proud of you. No. He would not have been. But he would have wanted to be. And for me, because I love him, and because I have outlived the inhibitions he imposed, that is enough.

Varieties of Fiction

WHEN MY THEN-FOURTEEN-YEAR-OLD DAUGHTER asked if she could read my newly published collection of stories, I hesitated, because of her language-based disabilities. Several of the pieces involve parents struggling with their sorrow over their disabled children's challenges, struggling to adjust. Though not autobiographical, these accounts are echoes of my own experiences, and my first impulse was to protect her from reading that. But she was in a phase of feeling keenly that we had babied her for her entire life, of accusing us of defining her by what she cannot do. And she campaigned hard. So, after that initial hesitation, I gave her a copy of her own.

She carried it from room to room for several days while I stood at the ready, prepared to have whatever conversation seemed necessary. She sat with it, held it open now and then, and turned the pages—though not entirely convincingly. And gradually, I realized that there might be more pretending than actual reading going on, that it wasn't the content that would upset her, but her inability to penetrate the words.

"You don't have to read that, you know," I said, as I watched her try.

"I know," she said.

"Those stories can be hard to understand. Even for grown-ups."

"I know," she said again, her gaze steady on the page, everything about her posture a plea that I let the subject go.

I sometimes picture all those words I write, the letters, the punctuation marks, the ink itself, as a curtain of thick, black lace, through which my daughter cannot see. And at such moments, I hate the work that gives me so much pleasure, hate myself for thickening that curtain, for bolstering her sense that there is something very beautiful beyond her view.

For days it seemed as though every time I walked into the room, she picked up the book. For days, I could sense in these actions, in her body, in a kind of nervous force field surrounding her, that she didn't trust me not to pin her down on what she had—or hadn't—read. And she wasn't wrong to be concerned. For years, I have thought of denial as harmful, as weak. Many writers do. We view ourselves as truth-tellers and find virtue in that role. My daughter knows me well.

But then, the book disappeared into her room. "I loved your stories," she told me soon after that. "They're really good."

Once upon a time, I would have insisted it was healthiest to pierce whatever pretense might be at work. But even I have gradually come to understand what life has forced my child to grasp from early on, that it is a luxury to insist on blunt honesty as always best, a luxury to be granted an existence in which denial's softening mercies are not necessary now and then.

"Thank you," I said. "That means a great deal to me."

Encouraging a lie? Perhaps. Or maybe just acknowledging that there are fictions far more important than my own.

II. WRITING (& LIFE)

Twenty-One Things I Wish I'd Known Before I Started to Write

1. PUBLICATION DOESN'T MAKE you a writer. Publication makes you a published writer. Writing makes you a writer.

2. Your "writer friends" are suddenly going to seem a lot more interesting, understanding, *simpatico,* and just plain fun than the friends (and sometimes family) you had before you threw yourself into this pursuit. I mean, they *get* you! But be gentle with the ones who were there all along—and remember the support they've given you, and the care; and try not to hurt their feelings by making it clear how much more compelling the ones who "speak writer" now seem. (And may not always seem…)

3. The best you can do is the best *you* can do. There's a fine line between learning from other authors and trying to be them. Be yourself. There are more than enough different types of readers out there for us all. I can't tell you how much time I have wasted wishing my work were "hipper" and "edgier." And every single moment was indeed a waste of time. I didn't even like much of the writing I wanted to emulate. I just liked the attention heaped on the people who wrote it. Write the book you'd most like to read—not the one you think will win over the editor *du jour.*

4. Not everyone will love your work. Not everyone will like your work. Some people will hate your work. Don't put energy into pursuing the fantasy of universal adoration. It has nothing to do with writing and everything to do with guaranteeing that you'll never be satisfied.

5. Don't expect yourself not to be jealous, but don't let yourself act on it. Be jealous and be generous. Be jealous and *feel* generous.

6. You will make mistakes. You will seem too pushy. You will seem falsely humble. You will forget someone in your acknowledgments. You will rush publication on something not ready to go. You will say things to your editor you'll wish you hadn't said. You'll accept edits you shouldn't accept. You'll give a friend unhelpful advice on a draft. You'll forget to read a draft you promised you'd read. You'll ask for one favor too many. Don't expect perfection of yourself. Do your best. Feel bad when you screw up, apologize, and don't let it make you hate yourself. A lot of writers seem awfully prone to self-hatred. Try to cut yourself some slack.

7. But be vigilant about being a jerk. We all make mistakes—but it's also frighteningly easy to become a taker, a user, a self-absorbed neurotic wreck, and not even know that's what you've become. Don't be too hard on yourself, but don't assume you haven't fallen into bad-colleague practices either.

8. Many writers live in bubbles. It could be family. It could be editors, friends, an admiring workshop. Your bubble loves you and loves your work. Your bubble may give you inflated ideas about the impact your work is going to have on the universe. Before you step into the great big world, try to remember that the world may not receive your work the way your bubble has. Try not to let yourself be set up for a huge

disappointment. It's such a privilege to have readers at all—don't undermine the joy of that privilege by setting your sights so high you forget to feel grateful.

9. Speaking of which, know what counts as success for you. If it's the New York *Times* bestseller list, then know that. If it's the grudging respect of a former lover, own it. If it's critical acclaim and not so much about sales, try to remember that fact. There are cultural templates of ambition—prizes, lists, etc.—that the world will tell you count as success. But don't fall for believing that they're necessarily what *you* want. Only a very few writers get those things, so if that's all that counts as success for you, you're just setting yourself up to fail.

10. If you have kids, don't insist that *your* career be the center of *their* lives. It's more than enough if they're engaged and happy when good things happen for you. It's not their job to see your artistic life as the center of their home. They may even push back a little bit. Kids are smart. They know what's competing with them for your attention and they aren't always going to welcome their rivals. Nor should they. I grew up in a home where a parent's career was in many ways the emotional center of the household; and trust me, it's a lousy way to grow up.

11. If you have success of any kind, don't believe your own hype. Maintain a little skepticism about your "victory." The most inspiring authors to me are those who respect their own work, and are even proud of it, but don't give off an air of entitlement, don't act like they've been owed that seven-figure book deal since birth.

12. Network only as much as you can bear. Don't obsess about your followers or your platform. Time spent on platform cultivation is almost

always time better spent writing. If you enjoy Twitter, that's one thing, but if you don't, then skip it. As much as publishers say they love authors with platforms, no extraordinary book has ever been rejected because of a lack of a Twitter following. And if you're doing it to sell books? People would love to think Twitter sells books, because then we'd all know something that sells books; but the internet is littered with people who made splashy online names for themselves and then had sales numbers that still keep them up nights wondering what the hell went wrong.

13. Don't suck up to famous writers so they'll blurb your book—the one you wrote that's soon to be published, or the one you're sure you will write one of these days. I didn't ever do that; but then at a certain point (big confession) I kind of wished I had. And now I'm very glad I never did. It's just icky. Plus, they know you're doing it.

14. It isn't in the power of an editor (agent, etc.) to tell you whether or not you're a writer. It's that person's job only to tell you if they want to work with you and your manuscript. Don't view rejections as the final word on your worth—or even on the worth of the pages that were returned. You are the only person who gets to decide if you're a writer or not.

15. Before you decide that someone will reject your work, give them the opportunity to do so. You might be shocked by who falls madly in love with what you wrote.

16. If your Goodreads, Amazon, etc. review of a friend's book is going to lower their average, don't review the book. Your integrity as a literary community member does *not* require you to make things harder for your friends. And if you loved the book, consider taking the two minutes it takes to tell the world.

17. There are only so many manuscripts you can read for free before you begin to resent the people who are sending them to you. Try not to get in the habit of doing "favors" that tick you off. Find a way, when it's appropriate, to make a reading fee clear—or just say you don't have time. It's not doing anyone a favor to read a draft with steam coming out of your ears. When you offer to read a manuscript, do it because you want to be a help to a friend, or because the project interests you, and not because you haven't learned how to say "no."

18. Annnd…don't ask people to read and comment on your work for free—unless you gave them a kidney (or read their book for them). But, if they offer, don't hesitate to accept. Take them at their word, and offer to reciprocate if that's ever a help.

19. You cannot write the pages you love without writing the pages you hate. Nothing that you write is pointless, useless, or unnecessary. The product requires the process. The good days may be more enjoyable, but the tough ones are the ones they're built upon.

20. Don't believe there are rules. There is only advice. There is only opinion. There are only my experiences and yours and yours and yours…

21. Make your skin as thick as you are able to, for your career. Keep it as thin as you can tolerate for your art.

The Collaborative Reader

IT IS A MAGIC trick: I make people up, events, locales—and, as I do, I trap those fancies in little black squiggles on a page where they remain, inert, until a reader uses her imagination to free them—though in an altered form. My story becomes our story, because writing, it turns out, is a collaborative act.

Others have noted this fact. In his essay "The Half-Known World," in the book of the same name, Robert Boswell writes: "The illusion of people and place created by a story is the algebraic product of a writer's art and a reader's engagement." That seems indisputable, and since no two readers are alike, all works of fiction therefore have at least as many versions as readers. "At least" because a person who rereads will inevitably create a slightly different story the second time through.

When I started writing, I didn't understand that the creation of a story involves a reader's active participation. I envisioned readers as passive observers to my performance in wordsmithery. I was doing something, and they were having it done to them. I was holding forth and they were listening. I was showing off and they were admiring. I was laying down the law, and they were taking note. If I said a character died, the character died. If I said the sky was blue, it was blue.

Which is almost true, but not quite. Those two assertions, the unfolding of an event and the color of the sky, do not reach a reader with the same authority—because the story doesn't belong to me alone. It belongs to me and to every reader. We have distinct roles, and we have distinct responsibilities.

If I say a thing happened, it did. If I write that a woman gave birth to twins, there's really no argument. But if I say the sky is blue, my authority is immediately tempered by the reader's imagination. I cannot dictate what shade of blue the reader pictures. Or the other reader. Or the next. It doesn't matter the detail in which I describe the sky, its hue. It doesn't matter how many metaphors I spin, robin's eggs, stained glass, I cannot control what goes through a reader's head.

The woman had twins. Because I said so. The sky is robin's egg blue. Whatever that means to you.

These two strands intertwine throughout every work of fiction: First, that which is mine, the author's, to assert without modification and then, that which is a reader's to invent, using the author's words as a starting place. The house has seven rooms. Mine. The house smelled of soup. Not mine. The car went off the bridge. Mine. As the car went off the bridge Frank experienced a loneliness so keen it felt like a new state of consciousness. Not mine.

Just the facts, ma'am. Anything subject to the least bit of interpretation belongs as much to the reader as to me, and nowhere is this knowledge as important as at the beginning of a story and at its end.

What happens at the start of a story? If everything goes as hoped, the reader falls into an imaginative state—not unlike that of the writer when writing—ready to play her role in making the story up. She gives her imagination over to the service of the words on the page. She is no longer exactly in the room she occupies, not exactly in the time that passes through her. Many call this the dream state. Whatever one calls it, I find it infinitely moving that two strangers can occupy an imaginary world together, apart from all else. Can, in fact, make that world up together, apart from all else.

But there are ways to disrupt the process, making it harder for a reader to let go of reality. The mistake of asking the reader to jump too quickly to the thread of the fiction that belongs to her lies at the heart of many such failures. The blue sky. The musty smell of the house.

The particular shine of a mirror. The smile reflected in that mirror. If a reader is asked to do too much of the work at the start, to imagine rather than learn too many elements all at once, the spell cannot take hold.

There is a necessary seduction that must take place before a reader's imagination can be fully engaged. She must know something before she can imagine much. She must be oriented before she can wander on her own, must be secure in the author's authority before she can begin to challenge it.

There is no perfect balance of course, no formula for this—and no rules. In reality, my "musts" are wispy assertions, subject to challenge, as are all "musts" when applied to writing. But understood as such, they can form a useful lens through which to examine the dynamics of a story's opening.

The process of crafting fictions is in large part a process of manipulating that which is subject to modification by the reader's imagination and that which is not. Invitations to imagine punctuated by undeniable facts. And beginnings of stories are very often suited for the sort of clarity that puts a reader in a maximally passive role, the author in charge, if only for a very short time, if only for a few sentences, a few words, if only to bring about the surrender that is necessary at first.

These notions apply to endings as well, where once again those two strands—the author's to assert, the reader's to imagine—separate. Because conventional stories don't have a single ending, but two. There is the resolution of the plot which is the responsibility of the author, and then there are the words that follow that resolution, up to the final words on the final page.

I first heard this theory of double endings in a lecture given by Steven Schwartz. He used the term "fulcrum" to describe that point at which the storyline is resolved and begins a slide into its literal ending. I have come to think of that fulcrum as the point at which the author steps away from the absolutes of plot, over which she has full authority, and begins to give the story to the reader to take away.

An example: The central problem of a story is whether or not a couple will get back together. On the top of page twenty-one, the author asserts that they do. They have reunited. No room for disagreement. But then there is another page or so, a stretch of language in which the author seems to loosen her grip, allowing for more and more interpretation. The sentences are more about atmosphere and mood than event. A metaphor may be introduced. The future may be referenced if only briefly, suggesting a time outside the author's ken. And as the question of "what happens" recedes, the burden shifts to the reader to begin the process of interpretation, a process that will continue long past the final words. With this shift, what the author held in her imagination, before trapping it onto the page, is entirely transferred to another's imagination, transformed in the process, recognizable still.

And in the course of the transfer, the author loses control. Even the events of the story, hers to determine, take on a new life as their meaning is mined and worried through. The reader becomes trustee not only of what the author imagined, but of the uncertainty underlying it. Their roles have been blurred, are intersecting, overlapping, indistinct, as the reader continues the process of writing long after the author has stopped.

I had no idea, when I started to write, that the best possible result of hours at the keyboard, years at the keyboard, would be this relinquishment, this acceptance of another's role in creating what had once seemed so certainly to be mine. But by now I have heard readers argue about my characters as if they were real people, making claims about them that were far from my intent, not even asking me for my view. And for all that my ego may desire a kind of ownership over my creations, there is simply no greater honor, no greater joy, than understanding that it is safe to step away.

The Final Draft:
What's Love Got to Do With It?

IN 1993, MY FIRST marriage failed—eight years and two children in—and over the months, the years, that followed, I took on a strange, unanticipated role: advisor to the unhappily wed. *How did you know?* they would quiz me, at toddlers' birthday parties, at school assemblies. *How did you know to end it?* they would ask as we shepherded our Power Rangers, our witches, down dark suburban Halloween streets.

How did you know when to call it quits?

It didn't take me long to realize that I wanted no part in advising other people about whether or not to end their marriages. I had experienced too thoroughly the inability of any outsider to understand such a relationship and I knew too well how much was at stake. But there was one piece of advice I always felt comfortable giving: *If you decide to leave,* I would say, *be sure you can articulate to yourself exactly why you chose to go, because I promise you there will be times when you doubt your choice, and you will need to have a very clear set of reasons to recite to yourself during those shaky days.*

That makes sense, they would say—disappointed, I knew, at the neutrality of my response.

Soon enough, I remarried, and people stopped thinking of me as a poster child for getting-divorced-when-you-have-little-kids, so I heard those questions less and less. But then I took up writing, then started teaching writing, and I began to hear other questions, oddly resonant of those.

How do you know when a story is finished? How do you know when it's time to send a story out?

How do you know when to call it quits?

It took me a while to realize that the answer I always give to this question is itself an echo of the other, earlier one: *I know a story isn't finished until I can explain to myself exactly why I have made all the craft choices I have made.*

Or, to put it another way, if you plan on ending your relationship to a story and exposing it to the harsh gaze of those who didn't write it, you had better be able to articulate to yourself why you think it's time, because there are likely to be times when you doubt that you should have done so.

I have long searched for any kind of scaffold on which I can hang an understanding of the role of intent in the process of writing, of how it evolves, ebbs and flows, and finally dominates through draft after draft after draft. In the past, I've always told students that first drafts should be as much like vomiting as possible, but I think (and this is happy news for future students) that I will now start saying instead that first drafts are like falling in love. *Letting go. Giving in. Following a hunch. Obsessing. Hoping. Fantasizing. Knowing fuck-all about what's going on.* The vocabularies of early drafting and of nascent romance are essentially interchangeable. Even the presence of an irresistible erotic force connects the two.

And mystery. It is all about mystery at the start. If we premised losing our hearts on our ability to explain doing so, we'd none of us ever lose our hearts. And, for many of us, it's also true that if we stop too long to try and understand our early drafts, we may well find we have indeed stopped too long. At the start of both relationships, something bordering on lunacy is a necessary state.

But then, you show the story to a trusted reader who makes some imperfection in it clear. (*You introduce your beloved to your best friend and realize in her company that he laughs too loudly, too long at his own jokes.*) You approach the next draft with this flaw in mind, engaging your intellect exactly as you *couldn't* do while drafting. (*You ponder if there is tact enough in the world to suggest to him that he not convey to others how amusing he finds himself to be.*) In writing and in romance, it is both impossible and inadvisable to maintain eternally the state of insanity necessary to get the thing going at the start.

And the hope is, in both pursuits, that even that initial lunatic state will become a little less crazy with experience. The next time you meet a potential love, you may be a bit cannier about what endearing traits will ultimately drive you mad. And in writing, an analogous goal motivates us to study craft, in the hope that some of it will become second nature even when we're in a fevered state.

But the analogy isn't exact, of course. No genuinely helpful analogy—or metaphor—ever is. (What would be the evocative power of comparing identical phenomena?) Here, the comparison begins to fail around the word "failure" itself. When you leave a marriage it is because it has failed; when you send a story out it is because you believe that it succeeds. For better and worse, we have built into our cultural understanding of marriage that it isn't meant to be perfect—for better *and* worse—that it cannot be perfect, and that to insist on perfection is to doom the union; but writers *do* strive for perfection. Even those of us who know in our hearts that we'll never get it entirely "right," even those of us who claim to value a little mess in literature, cherish fantasies of perfection while caught up in a piece—necessarily, I suspect, if quixotically too. That is, unless we let impatience rule the day.

In the aftermath of my divorce, there were many occasions when I saw the pain it caused my children and I needed that list of all the reasons it had been the right thing to do. My silent catechism got me through some very shaky times.

But I wasn't always so fortunate or so prudent with my work. In that realm, I have been burned by cutting corners. I once sent out a story knowing, knowing, that I didn't understand why I had ended it the way I had, and that it might well not be right, that it probably wasn't right; and that suspicion rubbed at me like sandpaper. But being new to the game and desperate for some "success" I decided to take a shot anyway, and it was accepted for publication.

When the journal arrived at my door, I wanted to rip those pages out. When friends told me they had read it, I wanted to apologize for all it didn't accomplish. When people praised it, I longed to explain why they were wrong. But then, as with old lovers who part too soon, only to meet again and make it work, I had the chance to rewrite that story for my book, and could give it the ending I could explain to myself, the one that justified my letting go. I could finally compose for myself a list of all the reasons behind the choices I had made.

No, the analogy isn't perfect. But I see enough here, enough to build on, enough, for sure, to spare the next class of students that image of vomiting onto the page—which always gets a good laugh, but also a recoil—and replace it with images of crazy, crazy, ill-fated love.

How (Not?) to Query

WHEN I'M ASKED FOR advice about querying agents, I'm always torn about what to say. There's a part of me that believes in playing such things safe, in following the rules, and not raising any "cuckoo-bird" flags. So with that in mind, I'm tempted to refer people to the many websites about the "proper" way to query, websites where they will find advice about being succinct; about crafting catchy, brief summaries of their work; about trying to sound appealing, exhibiting *some* personality but still striking a professional tone.

All of which is probably excellent advice, and none of which is what I did. Hence my dilemma.

A couple of summers after completing my MFA, I had a passel of published stories to my name, and I decided I "needed" an agent. (For the record, if anyone with that résumé were now to ask me for advice, I would say: *Don't bother querying agents until you have a book. Write first, and stay out of the business side as long as possible.*) Like many "emerging writers" and perhaps especially those no longer young, I was in a hurry. I wanted legitimacy. I wanted to be able to say, "Yes! Indeed, I do," when people asked me: "Do you have an agent?"—one of the inquiries people mistakenly use to measure a writer's worth.

But nothing came of those agent queries in 2007, which were pretty much "by the book," following the rules I found online. Nothing came of them, including the one I cared most about, to a man named Henry Dunow. He was the agent on whom I had fixated, absolutely convinced he was the one for me—for no better reason than that someone had once told me he might be a good match for my work. In passing. At a weekend convention. Probably while drunk. And never having read my work. "You should work with Henry Dunow. He's into your kind of stuff. *Hic.*"

I was unimaginably impressionable back then. A drunk dude told me that Henry Dunow was the agent for me, and it became an *idee fixe*.

But he didn't answer my email. Fair enough. He wasn't the only one. As I said, nothing came of the whole enterprise, and I went back to work.

Flash forward a year, and through a series of incidents, some involving more stories, others involving the kindness of an "insider" who decided to help me, and suddenly I had agents returning my emails—in part because I had managed to produce a novel draft, which I was careful to mention two times for every time I mentioned my short stories. A couple of these folks seemed like real possibilities, but an *idee fixe* is an *idee fixe*, and I decided that before I signed with anyone else, I would give Henry Dunow one more try.

But something had changed in a year. Maybe because my by-the-book emails had all failed, maybe because I had just grown weary of trying to play by the rules, my tone had, shall we say, evolved.

Here, in part, is the email that I sent:

"This is where I fess up that I wrote you last summer. Since I didn't hear back, I'm assuming that's because you decided against me, but I'm hoping it's because the email never reached you. I am trying again—for the last time, I promise—because your blurb on the agency's website says you like literary fiction and voice driven nonfiction, and that is what I write. Since the One Story *piece came out, I have had some interest from agents, and it looks like the right time for me to figure this representation thing out, so I thought I would try one more time.*

"I apologize if this second query letter qualifies as bugging you. As I say, I won't send another should this one also go unanswered. My bio is pasted below. I am happy to give you any more information, including a description of the novel, should you want it."

Professional tone? Not hardly. Catchy summary of my work? Definitely not. Gratuitous reference to the possibility that I'm a stalker? Yeah, I can see that there.

The miracle is that he wrote back. Not only did he write back, but he asked if he could take a look at my novel, a reasonable enough request, given that I had told him it was complete.

My answer:

"Thanks so much for the response! I appreciate that, and your willingness to look at my work.

"Unfortunately, as far as you seeing the novel goes, the short answer is no. Though fully drafted, I don't think the novel is showable—not without doing myself a disservice and wasting your time."

(This move, the dangling of a novel followed by its hasty withdrawal, is not commonly advised.)

My email continues:

"It's a good thing I am a better writer than businesswoman. I had actually decided to put off querying until those revisions were complete, but my situation is that a couple of weeks ago this story of mine came out in One Story *and all of a sudden there were agents offering to sign me up, which was initially incredibly exciting. Now though, after a certain amount of soul searching, I'm coming to the view that flattering and tempting as it all is, I don't just want to sign with an agent, I want to sign with the right agent. I understand that may mean someone for whom the novel is the determining factor, therefore a wait."*

I am 100% certain that nowhere in the literature on How To Query An Agent does anyone suggest that you discuss your "soul searching."

There's more:

"I so appreciate your response. My now revised query is whether I could show you this novel once that too is revised? Or is there anything else that would be relevant? Do stories help? I have lots and lots of those, some published,

some (too many) that I have never sent out. I am attaching the story that appeared in One Story, *just so if you are interested in seeing a sample of my work, there it is. And of course, anything that might be useful can be mailed in the genuine mail if that's better. Also, below is a description of the novel. The only person in the industry who has ever heard anything about it told me that you were the right agent, because of your experience and skill selling literary work. That doesn't mean you would agree, of course, but it had an impact on me...*"

And yes, in case you are wondering as you read, I am *still* cringing. And I'm not even going to share the next email I sent in which I apologize for the previous two and for being such a complete idiot and so on...

Amazingly enough, Henry didn't run screaming or change his email address or mark my missives spam. He just wrote back, "*Okay. I'll take a look at the story and get back to you,*" which I assumed meant he was being polite about trying to get rid of me, but in fact resulted in an email a couple of days later inviting me to give him a call so we could speak. And the rest is history. Not world history, but the part of my history that includes having a terrific agent and friend.

That happy ending isn't really the point here, though. The important part of this story is not that Henry wanted to work with me once he'd read my work, it's that he read my work in spite of the decidedly unprofessional tone of my correspondence, in spite of my having broken every rule in the book. The most pressing goal of a query letter isn't that it result in being *signed*; it's that it result in being *read*.

So what advice am I to give?

I had a chance to go to the expert and ask Henry himself why he bothered to download that story and take a look.

"I remember being charmed," he said. "You sounded like a real person."

"A real nut," I said, but he only shrugged.

And what I understood, then, is that my story isn't as fluky as I have always believed. Agents aren't all looking for one thing. They are human beings, after all. So there are agents out there—and I'm not saying it's the majority—who *aren't*, first and foremost, looking for authors who can mimic a professional tone and sound like business-people. Instead, they may be looking for that ever elusive quality: *voice*. Or personality. There are agents who don't expect writers to sound 100% balanced all the time—or ever; agents who may very well be bored to death by the dozens of "by the book" queries they receive every month.

So my advice, when it comes to query letters, is: Be yourself. Let a process of natural selection work itself out. Being neurotic, tentative, and entirely unprofessional got me the agent who was right—for me. One who doesn't mind a little craziness along the way. One who may even welcome that. There are surely agents who would have deleted that first loopy email that I sent, barely read—and that would have been a very good thing for us both.

Line Edits I

JULIETTE THEN ASKED SARA about the house that the families were hoping to buy.

Juliette then asked her about the house that the families were hoping to buy.

Juliette asked about the house the families were hoping to buy.

Juliette asked about the house the families hoped to buy.

She asked about the house the families hoped to buy.

Juliette asked about the house they hoped to buy.

Juliette asked about the house. "What's the place like?"

"What's the house like?" Juliette asked.

"What's the house like?" she asked.

"What's the house like?"

Living in the Present

WHEN I SENT THE last story for my collection to my agent, he soon called with his approval. I was thrilled. *Hooray!! The manuscript is complete!* But within minutes my joy was marred by an unshakable sense that there was still something wrong. "You know, I think I should throw the story into present tense," I said before we ended the call. "I think it makes sense for this one."

It was a concession of sorts for me. Not so long before, I had claimed to despise present tense—a fairly common claim. For many people present tense is a love-it-or-hate-it kind of thing, almost as though it were some kind of isolated element, distinct from the integrated whole of the story—a bit like cilantro.

I would have loved the salsa, except it had cilantro in it. That makes some sense.

It was a terrific story except I hate present tense. That one, not so much.

One of my newest crusades is to convince the world that there are no bad craft elements, only poor uses of them. In other words, cilantro may always taste like cilantro, but present tense need not carry the same flavor every time.

The Case Against Present Tense

Having asked some of the haters why they hate, I've often heard words like "stilted" and "robotic." (And in fact have used them myself.) People hear a sameness in the tone of present tense stories. That tone comes from a particular sentence structure that can sound like detached, dispassionate reportage. *Samantha walks to the window. She raises the shade. She stands there and stares outside for a time.* It's a style that can evoke stage directions. It's been used to great effect in some second person stories to mimic the form of instruction manuals. (See Lorrie Moore's "How To Be An Other Woman.") But when there's no inherent reason in a story for the rigidity of sentence after sentence with that same basic structure, it can have the impact of making otherwise disparate stories begin to sound alike.

I suspect that many of the people who have tired of that particular tone, and claim to hate all fiction in present tense, have also read a lot of present tense stories without even registering that they have.

As she walks to the window, Samantha trips over a ball of yarn, so at first she reaches for the shade's cord only to steady herself. But then, after a moment, she pulls on it purposefully. Free from further worries about what treacherous objects might be strewn on the floor, she stands there for a time and stares outside.

I'll admit, I've added a lot here, but in a sense that's the point. I think of these additional clauses and details as softening agents, meant not only to convey the scene, as any such passages are, but also to minimize awareness of my choice of tense. The sentence structure is varied, no longer beginning with the subject followed by a verb, which helps, but perhaps less obviously, Samantha's actions are now connected by something other than the fact that *she* did them all. She trips *while* walking to the window and she holds onto the cord *because* she tripped. Timing and causation come into play, and, subtle though those elements are, they provide a gravitational pull away from a consciousness of the tense in which it's all being told. In other words, a present tense story need not always register as a present tense story.

But why bother at all? Even if you can keep present tense from sounding stilted, are there positive reasons to choose it?

The Case for Present Tense

To go back to the story that I redrafted in 2009, my decision to shift tenses in that instance was based on the fact that my central, point of view character—Jeremy—was chronically befuddled. The point of view in that story is close, and there was a way in which telling it as though it had all happened some time back, as though it were settled history, seemed at odds with his bewilderment. I had a hunch that putting it into present tense would dovetail well with the sense I wanted to create that he never knew what might happen next. People often talk about the "immediacy" of present tense, a term that is generally used to describe the reader's relationship to the story. But tense can also have its basis in the level and type of knowledge you want your point of view character to have.

For example, as soon as a first person narrator begins to tell a story in past tense, questions arise about the length of time that has elapsed between the events of the story and its telling. *What does the narrator know, as she recounts, that she didn't know when those events were unfolding? Why is the narrator choosing to tell this story "now"?* All of these questions can lead to the right kind of complexity for a story, but sometimes they just get in the way. A first person story told in present tense is a strange conceit, almost as though the narrator were both acting and recounting her actions at once, but, when well-executed, it cuts out the need to account for all the circumstances surrounding the retrospective narrator.

Present tense can also be useful when you are going to have a great deal of "back story" to manage. It's not impossible to distinguish the past from the more distant past, we have an entire tense designed to do just that. But there are times when it is just simpler and clearer to have the "front story" in present tense and the "back story" in past. If nothing else, it saves a lot of fiddling around with past perfect which while obviously worth doing sometimes, at other times seems to muddy as much as it elucidates.

The truth is that present tense is no more or less constricting than past. It has its purposes and its limitations. And, as with so many other writing elements, the choice of tense for a story has more to do with the best way to tell that particular story than with whether in the abstract one prefers one form of storytelling over another.

Which isn't a bit like cilantro at all. Speaking as someone who loves cilantro.

If Only! The Imaginative Wealth of What Didn't Take Place

THERE IS A CONNECTION between regret and fiction writing—even beyond the obvious possibility that one might regret ever having started to write fiction.

Regret is among a very few emotions that cannot exist without an accompanying narrative. *I wish I had gone on that trip because...I then would have met the love of my life; I then wouldn't have set the house on fire; I then would have seen Paris before I died, which would have made dying more bearable for me.* All regret carries within it a particular kind of story, one in which the rules of causality and chance are suspended—generally in favor of a happy ending. We who know that we *cannot* know what any future moment might bring convince ourselves that we *can* know what would have happened in the past...*if only*. Regret makes confident storytellers of us all.

It also makes us fans of bold action—retrospectively, anyway. Social scientists and psychologists are agreed that people are more likely to regret what they have *not* done than what they *have* done. Since that concept of 'doing' and 'not doing' is a slippery one—when you *don't* go on the trip you *do* stay home—I take this to mean that people tend to feel regret when they *perceive* that they have failed to do something more often than when they *perceive* that they have actively done the wrong thing. It's the missed opportunity that feels poignant. The road not taken. The challenge to which we do not rise. The one who got away. These are the regrets that engender most of the poignant, private literature of what might have been.

Inaction, it turns out, is a strangely rich source for the imagination, a fact that I have found to be of help when I am struggling with a story that has taken on a moribund, fruitless quality—as happens all too often. My narrative, once brimming with life and promise, has died—sometimes quite suddenly. There are many reasons for this, but one of the biggest impediments to reviving such work is too great a focus on what has happened in the story up to that point, as opposed to what has not.

As regret narratives so well demonstrate, what characters failed to do may actually be a more productive resource for imaginative thinking than what they did. More and more, when I hit that still and frightening place in my work, instead of pushing forward as I used to try to do, continuing from where I last wrote, I go back, convinced that I will find a missed opportunity in the text, gloriously brimming with *might have beens*. I look for lines like: I thought of telling him what had happened the night before, but decided against it. Or, *I could have run after her and pleaded my case, but instead, I went back inside.* Or, *She stared at the phone for a very long while, but never picked it up.* I hunt for the points of inaction that my characters might themselves later regret, those decisions that might inspire in them the rich fictions of which we are all such gifted authors when we are sorry to have chosen the safer, less active of two possible paths.

There are of course those fictional beings whose inaction is a defining, essential quality, but more often, in my work, the failure of a character to act is the result of my authorial hesitation, my reluctance to move into plot complications, and not a result of my character's temperament. There can be a certain satisfaction in keeping early drafts relatively simple. The lure of completion alone is enough to guarantee the appeal of a plot that seems to move easily along. When I write, I have something like a heat sensor that can detect potential complexity, the difficult exchanges, the entanglements that might arise; and against all interests of the story, my first instinct is often to avoid such sparks and fires, tamping and tamping—until one day I sit down at the computer to find a narrative that has taken on a deathly, immobile quality.

Some time ago, during such a moribund period with my novel, I went back through the pages, and sure enough discovered a moment at which my central character chooses inaction over a more complicated course: "I thought of going over to Alison's house and seeing if I could help, but decided against it." I changed her mind, had her march across her property and into her neighbor's home, and that simple walk from one house to another led to a scene that opened the book up for me. The relationship between my narrator and her neighbor took on a new kind of intimacy—a difficult one, a messier one. My narrator had to face limitations in her own ability to empathize. She had to see the other woman in a new light.

The pressure I had initially avoided by keeping them apart, performed the trick of clarifying character and therefore determining actions, as pressure so often does.

Many years ago, a friend of mine showed me her MFA thesis-in-progress, a collection of stories. She knew that a number seemed to lose their energy and their focus along the way, and she wanted my advice. I discovered that in more than a few, when the going between two characters got tough, one of them would get into a car and drive away. "I wanted to avoid a fight." "I couldn't stand listening anymore." My friend had done what I so often do, choosing the path of least resistance for her characters, shying away from the difficult scene—difficult for her fictional creations, and difficult for her.

And that difficulty isn't limited to crafting thorny conversation between characters. I have gone back into stories and realized that I stopped someone from taking a trip only because I semi-consciously realized that I would have had to do research on the destination. Authorial laziness is not a particularly fertile creative vein, whatever form it takes.

In real life, we don't get to return to our twenties and step onto the airplane we were afraid to fly; or audition for the play that excited and scared us; or ask the beauty to dinner; or take the job in Boston, despite logistical concerns. What's done is done and all we can do is tell ourselves the intuitively well-crafted stories of what might have been.

But in fiction, what has been done can be undone and what hasn't been done can be done—and very often should be. No limitations. No excuses. And no regrets.

No Fool Like a Bold Fool

SOMEWHERE BETWEEN A MILLION and a billion years ago, when I was a sophomore at Sarah Lawrence College, I took a fiction writing workshop with the extraordinary Allan Gurganus. Allan set us to writing a story a week for the full year, an experience for which I've been grateful ever since, chiefly because it taught me not to be overly precious with myself about every word I jot down. There's just no way to produce at that rate and maintain the illusion that everything you write is very good.

We had many different sorts of prompts, different parameters for each assignment. I don't remember the exact prompt that led me to write a story about a nineteenth-century sheep farmer who took in a beautiful stranger, who, if memory serves, either baked him a loaf of bread or spun his copious wool into yarn, but I do remember the beautiful stranger's name: *Genevieve*.

I remember her name with a cringe—and will remember it that way all my days—because at a certain point, as she stood in his doorway, wrapped in her too-thin cloak, facing out toward the dark, snowy night, he spoke the immortal words: "You needn't leave, Genevieve."

(Read it out loud, if you are missing the point.)

Sadly, I didn't catch it before making my copies and distributing them to the class. Inevitably, my classmates did. I don't think any serious or lengthy teasing went on, but it was enough that a couple of people repeated the phrase with dramatic emphasis, and perhaps a few laughed. Maybe more than a few. I was mortified. I am still mortified. The thought of that sing-song rhyme still makes me cringe.

You needn't leave, Genevieve.

Did I mention that this was more than thirty years ago?

I assure you that in those three decades plus I have done a lot worse than write an inadvertent, inopportune rhyme. Yet this particular gaffe has a special power over me. And I think I know why that is.

One of the great virtues of Allan's class with its many imaginative prompts and oh-so-frequent assignments was that we were all forced out of our respective comfort zones. I was not then (though I might now be) inclined to write about nineteenth-century sheep farmers— or, maybe more to the point, about the origins of a Great Love. (I still struggle with that.) I am certain that going into workshop that day I not only felt all the usual worries about being "shot down" for lousy writing, I also felt the particular worry of someone who has tried something entirely new. And so, in the way of these things, feeling foolish about the rhyme became feeling foolish about the story which became feeling foolish about writing which became feeling foolish about ever having thought I could write, which was really just feeling like a fool.

There are reasons comfort zones are called what they are. But there are also excellent reasons to step out of them.

I'm aware that many of the people who read my fiction now do so with certain expectations. They think of me as writing a specific kind of story, usually big on what people call "interiority," not so high on high drama. I'm also aware that so-called realist short stories, in general, not just mine, are also often read with set expectations, particularly about their endings, which, to put it very crudely, include a kind of upward turn, an opening up of hope complete with a physical representation of optimism, the ray of sunshine just brushing the top of the glistening wheat field, pointing the way toward a brighter future…

Or anyway, whatever the merit of that gross generalization in the larger literature, when I was working on my collection of stories I felt myself in danger of writing too much and too automatically to that expectation. The "final lilt" as I thought of it. My loyalty to these endings seemed to me to be dishonest if my work was to reflect the human condition. I knew a family then who had been crushed by multiple tragedies all at once, and I knew that for them—as for many other inhabitants of this earth—there was no upward lilt to come, no moment of redemptive understanding. I decided that as an artist, I had an obligation to try to make art that took that possibility into account. Art that didn't braid itself to hope quite so tightly as my stories had done up until that point. Yes, those works had dealt with tragic situations more often than not, but they hadn't revealed the chasm of pure, unwavering tragedy that runs alongside all our lives. And so I set myself the challenge of writing a short story that was a complete bummer. But still a story. But still a bummer. But still good.

The result was the title story of my collection *If I loved you, I would you tell you this*—first published in the *Southern Review* as "A Fence Between Our Homes." And it is definitely a bummer. It is also, decidedly, not to everybody's taste. I spoke with more than one publisher about my collection before signing with the one I have, and while the editor who ultimately took the book told me that that story was what sold her on me, someone else who was interested in the collection added the caveat that the same story would have to be cut. "It's just too much. Too over the top. I'm sure you understand."

And both turned out to be right. Right, and in plenty of company. When the collection came out, it was the rare review that didn't single the title story out as either the high point or the low point of the book.

Years later, when writing my novel, I realized at a certain point that there was going to have to be an event in the book unlike anything else I'd ever written, definitely not something that fits in with the general tone of my previous work. Writing that part of the book felt risky to me, but necessary. To avoid writing it felt cowardly, choosing safety, choosing comfort, over what I believed to be artistically correct. So into unfamiliar territory I stepped...

And, sure enough, this element of the novel is the sequence most often singled out, by readers and reviewers both, as either the high or the low point of the book.

I recognize that what I've said here about the responses to those two works sounds pretty resigned, pretty thick-skinned. Some love my work, some hate it. *C'est la guerre.* But in fact, I have found the criticisms of these two examples to contain in them a spark of what I think of as my Genevieve Moment. I'm not only upset or bummed when someone hates that tragic story or says that this un-Robin-like element of my novel doesn't work, I also feel foolish. Because I know that I tiptoed onto unfamiliar ground. I presumed to try something new, and some noticeable percentage of the people who read those pages kind of wished I'd just done what they'd seen me do before. Maybe because this isn't what they read me for. Maybe because, unpracticed at what I attempted, I made mistakes. Maybe tucked into those moments of my bravery there are, unknown to me, inadvertent funny little rhymes—or an equivalent. Resonances of clunkiness, just where I was going for delicacy.

Criticism for something that feels risky has a particular quality to it, a potential to make me meeker about challenging myself next time.

Oh, never mind. It's back to muted drawing-room dramas for me…
Sorry about that.

But then I—we all—have to take the other side into account: the people for whom these experiments end up being the most powerful aspect of the work. I have to remember those readers, even though it is almost magically easy to let any criticism eclipse all praise. And I not only have to remember those people, I have to somehow imbue their encouragement with the same power, the same unique quality I so easily give to the detractors of the work. If the critics make me feel foolish for having tried, then those who appreciate the risks must have equal power to further embolden me.

And in fact, ideally, the voices of encouragement should not only balance those that are critical but negate them entirely. Not because one shouldn't ever to listen to constructive or helpful criticism, but because in the specific case of writing that takes you out of your comfort zone, there is no role for voices that try to push you back to where you feel safe.

No role. Hands over ears. *La-la-la-la-la-la….*

At some point, we probably all glimpse, even nurture, the fantasy of universal approval. But it is a better goal to evoke passion—even when it includes both extremes. On my good days, when my head is truly in the game, I would rather my work be adored by some and despised by others than that it be liked by all. That expansion of acceptable response allows me to take risks. And taking risks is the only way I can grow.

None of which means I didn't learn a lesson in 1982, way back when. For sure, I learned to read my work aloud—if only to make sure it doesn't rhyme. And maybe I also learned that it is possible to survive a little ridicule and live to write another day.

Give It Up

THE STORY BEGINS WITH Charlotte getting dressed. She changes three times, because today is a big day. She settles on an outfit and heads downstairs, where she snaps at her children, because—let's be clear—today is a big day, and maybe not in a good way. It's making her short-tempered. She calls her former husband and tries to engage him, but he has no patience with her—maybe, she realizes, because she hasn't told him that today is a big day. As she ponders this, she feels bad that she snapped at her kids, and thinks about how her mother used to beat her when she was a child. But she shakes those thoughts off and gets in her car. Some more stuff happens—during which she remembers again that today is a big day—and then eventually she arrives at a hospital. Where she feels terrible, as the reality of what's awaiting her looms large. She takes the elevator up to a ward in which her unconscious mother lies. And she signs some papers. The papers that will allow the hospital to remove her mother's life support, the mother who used to beat Charlotte when Charlotte was a child...And then she leaves the hospital, choosing not to watch her mother die.

The End.

In the course of my teaching career, I have seen countless stories with this essential structure, the secret withheld to the end. (In the course of my writing career, I have crafted more than a few.) Withholding turns out to be a huge temptation for many writers, even though this kind of withholding of key information is almost always a bad idea.

Here is what my meeting with the author would look like:

Me: "So, I was interested in the fact that you chose to withhold what made that day so special. Why'd you do that?"

Student: "I'm not sure. I guess I felt like it was more powerful as a surprise."

Me: "Couple things about that…"

Student: "I guess I was wrong."

Me: "Well, we've all done it, trust me. But there are definitely issues with withholding a key piece of information like that, especially when the point of view character would be thinking about it the whole time."

Student: "Huh. I hadn't really thought about that part."

Me: "No problem. There's no shame in learning new stuff. Anyway, if Charlotte is obsessing over signing those papers, and we have access to Charlotte's thoughts, it's a little hinky that we never know that she's thinking about it all the time."

Student: "Right, right."

Me: "That's just a very practical issue with withholding a fact when the point of view character is aware of it—especially if they are obsessing on it. That's when your reader feels manipulated—in a bad way. But the point of view thing isn't the only problem with doing that. What do you suppose would happen if your first sentence was, 'It was the day when Charlotte was going to sign the papers allowing the hospital to remove all life support from her mother?'"

Student(frowning): "I don't know. I guess my worry is that the reader wouldn't have anything to be curious about."

Me: "What about being curious about how Charlotte is dealing with all this? I mean, in this draft I had no idea why she snapped at her kids, or called her ex, but if I knew what was on her mind, all those things might be much more interesting…"

Student: "You're always saying our work should be surprising. I guess I thought this was a surprise."

Me: "The thing is, there's a difference between a story being surprising, and a story having a surprise in it…"

And so on. I have cast myself as teacher here, but I have been at the other end of this exchange more than once.

We writers are terrified that a reader won't turn from one page to the next—a reasonable concern. That page-turn is the *sine qua non* of success, and a secret can create the sort of curiosity that will keep someone hooked. But reading to find out a fact is very different from being immersed in a story. Though a secret may indeed keep pages turning, it is also often a distraction from the story itself. (Obviously whodunnits fall into a different category, but my students and I aren't generally writing those—though you never know.)

The reader consumed by curiosity is not truly reading those pages at all, but rushing through them to get to the reveal. And the author may not quite be writing those pages either. Using an absence of information to generate the majority of a story's narrative momentum can allow a writer to slack off on every other element.

What happens if the reader knows from the opening line where Charlotte is headed that day? First (and most frightening to any author) the reader needs a new reason to turn the pages. Something else of interest must replace the taunting of secrecy. The author needs to access why the story matters, what makes it compelling, beyond the parlor trick of satisfying a curiosity she has created. Very likely, Charlotte has to change. Having existed only as a vehicle for a mounting tension that does nothing to shed light on her character, she must now become something more like a real person, just as the story itself, which was primarily a riddle, must now become a real story.

It's impossible to exaggerate the degree to which a narrative's structure is formed by withheld—and dangled—information. The reader's curiosity about what is unsaid creates a kind of shadow-plot, one that is ultimately resolved, not by any actions within the narrative, but by the false dénouement: "And then the reader finds out the truth about the big day."

It's a result notable for its lack of emotional content, and notable too for being the identical resolution whatever the subject of the story. In this case, the reader's potential stake in Charlotte, her dilemma, her day, is completely overpowered by the intellectual experience of learning something. "Oh! That's what's been going on all this time." The story is solved—and arguably, stories should never be solvable, much less solved. Even when central problems or questions intrinsic to the story are resolved, a story only survives being read if some mystery remains for the reader to contemplate.

I have often thought about the ways in which writing is an inherently hubristic pursuit. Embedded in the lines of every composition is the author's presumptuous assertion that what she has to say is worth hearing, that what she asks you to care about is worth caring about. It is tempting for many of us to find ways to undercut that stance, battle the possibility of being thought arrogant, and maybe avoid the experience of discovering that our confidence is misplaced. Withholding key information may feel like it places the author in a superior position, the puppet-master, the riddle-teller, but in fact it is often the strategy of a writer who is afraid she has nothing of genuine importance to say.

"*It was the day that Charlotte was to authorize the hospital to take her mother off life-support…*"

Now what?

House Lessons II:
To Renovate, to Revise

WE HAD LIVED IN our home for sixteen years when we began a much-needed renovation in preparation for selling it a few years down the line. (And yes, it was in bad enough shape that we required that much lead time to get it pulled together.) The family home had long before crossed the all important boundary between shabby chic and shabby, the line between lived-in and unlivable. Our roof was leaking. Copiously. The exterior paint was peeling off, revealing colors that predated our ownership. Two ceilings on the second floor had actually caved in. The bathrooms were disconcertingly gloomy. A number of our rugs had been chewed by moths who turned out also to have colonized our couch. And the list goes on…

Certain decisions were easy. Fresh paint, a new roof. Get those pesky ceilings back over our heads where they belonged. But then there were other choices to make, including some choices we hadn't even realized we could make.

When we moved in, in 1995, we commissioned a beautiful, pine desk from a local Amish craftsman. We wanted something that would fit in with the rest of our décor—countryish—but would be equipped with such crazy newfangled things as a pull-out keyboard shelf and holes through which computer wires could go. (Way back in '95, kids, it wasn't so easy to find such a piece of furniture.) The desk was beautiful, and by the summer that we began readying ourselves to move, it was imbued with many wonderful memories. It was also huge.

And though pretty much unused for several years, it was Our

Desk, a piece we thought of as integral to our lives. But it was in the wrong place for our new design scheme, so we began moving it around. My husband and I hauled it from one end of a room to the other to make space for a little sitting area we wanted—and discovered that the desk didn't work at all on that side. So we cleared out part of another room, though we didn't really think it fit there either. We ran through a series of imperfect placements over the course of some weeks, until I thought of something that had never occurred to either of us.

"You know, if it doesn't fit in here anymore and nobody is using it maybe we should sell it or give it away…"

And the funny thing was, once I had said it, it was obviously true. We gave the desk to our local hospital thrift shop, and felt nothing but relief.

But that is furniture. That is not fiction.

While much about revision is difficult, nothing presents the same kind of challenge as when an element that has been there from the start no longer works. It may have taken me and my husband weeks to realize that our desk could—and should—go, but it has sometimes taken me years to understand that what's wrong with a story I'm writing is that the original conceit no longer has a place on the page.

An example: I begin writing a story about a boy struggling in woodshop class, working through his father issues with the teacher there, but before many drafts the story "wants to be" about a young woman teacher who knows them both, and the baby she gave up. She is taking up more and more room on the page, and the sections about her feel more urgent, more alive, than anything else. But now, the character of the boy's father, whom I once thought central, whom I have crafted with great care, has been rendered unnecessary. It takes me some time to see this, and when I do, I keep him anyway through a few misshapen drafts, because it's next to impossible for me to perceive him as vestigial. He was the lynchpin of the original idea. He was the spark.

Another example: I decide to write a story about a young woman with two cats who is romantically involved with her much older landlord. I put a lot of effort into writing about the cats, using them to set up a whole symbolic thread in the work. Eventually though the story "demands" that I focus on him instead, and on his relationship with his former wife. And those cats are a misdirection now—pulling away from the heart of the story, confusing the question of what's important. But it takes me two years even to see them as an element I might change. Of course, once I do, I then resist.

Logically, if the result of cutting or drastically changing those characters, those circumstances, is good for the story, there should be no sense of loss with revisions such as these. But the writing process is anything but logical, and my experience with stories that "insist" on being about something other than what I thought they would be, is that I fight and fight and fight against even considering that possibility, much less accepting it.

This is not the same phenomenon as clinging to a well-turned phrase or poetic passage. I'm not talking about so-called "darlings" here. My resistance to seeing that a story has grown away from my original idea isn't about being entranced with that idea. It's closer to a kind of panic, as though that early thought, "I want to write a story about…" is a moment of security I don't want to leave.

And that makes sense to me—illogical though the result may be. There is precisely one time during which a writer is ignorant of the challenges and failures and frustrations of any given story, and that is when the story is still only an idea for a story. Bright. Shining. Promising. Unblemished. Take every vestige of that moment of optimism from the work, and you are left with the mess of it all, with the reality of not having had a clue about what you were getting yourself into. You are bereft of the confidence you first felt when you were in charge.

But it is also true that, whatever my resistance to such changes, the stories of mine I value most are those that exhibited enough flexibility and enough strength along the way that nary a trace of my original idea exists. They are the stories that seemed to be partners in the process of their own creation, bullying me to give up my attachments, pushing me toward questioning my assumptions, teaching me along the way. These are the stories that outstripped my understanding of what I should do. Stories that pulled me away from the temptations and dangers of certainty.

Perhaps it is odd that when a story succeeds in my eyes, as those have, I am quick to credit the story itself with an intelligence. But throughout the revision process, it becomes so important to listen to what one has written as if it were a separate entity, that in memory it can feel as though it was. And in reading the stories you are proudest of, it can feel oddly as though you, the author, were less their creator than you were the recipient of gifts with origins you don't understand. In letting go of your own assumptions, there can be wonderful rewards.

As of course there were for us with our desk—which I barely ever think about anymore. Though I do still keep a picture of that room, beautiful, reimagined, come into its own since that vestige of our distant past was removed.

Revising Reality

I RECENTLY READ AN article about reality, a physics theory I cannot even pretend to understand. The degree to which I don't understand it is itself kind of enjoyable, an intellectual free fall without a net. Not that being baffled is a rare experience for me—math, anyone?—but taking a few minutes to be actively baffled about the nature of existence, trying to wrap one's head around a specific bizarre hypothesis, is inherently different, trippy, requiring a letting-go that isn't just about giving up on "doing sums" or accepting never being able to spell *restaurant* without auto-correct. There's an enjoyment in the inability to comprehend— right up until it all makes me flip out.

And now, having admitted that I don't understand the theory at all, I will proceed to sum it up. Basically, the idea is that bunches of realities exist all at once and sometimes intersect. Not only are we not alone in the universe—old news—but we are not even close to the only version of our own reality. (Whoa!…and um, sure…I guess?) For example, one of two scenarios given by a physicist for a potential alternate reality was that it was the Portuguese who colonized Australia, not the British.

Mind-blowing! The Portuguese? In Australia??

No, wait. Really? That's all you've got? The notion of European colonization remains intact, just the politics play out a little differently? What about the story where humans only exist in Australia? What about the one where we all just get along???

It's not a physicist's job, I suppose, to come up with compelling storylines, but it's still striking to me how little liberty that physicist took with the storyline we already know. Striking, and also familiar, reminiscent of the superficial tinkering many of us do when fictionalizing a story we think of as true. (A note: Every writer should read Tim O'Brien's "How To Tell A True War Story." I am not talking about war stories here, and wouldn't presume to try. I'm talking about the kind of story about which people say, "That would make a good story.")

Many of us have been there. You start writing a story because something happened in real life that interests you, or that just seems like a good yarn. And you don't want to change it—even when trusted readers suggest that it might benefit from a change, even when you suspect that those readers are correct. And beyond not *wanting* to change it, you may be in the grips of the kind of unaware failure of imagination those physicists display, as if shackled by unseen forces to what you know to be "true."

But truth of that kind is no defense in fiction. A story that isn't fully realized, or that fails to convince its readers, can't be saved by a footnote explaining that it's based on fact. Perhaps ironically, one of the most common critiques of such works is that they are implausible. "I didn't believe she would shoot that cat," a reader says. "Nobody would do that." And the author protests, "Except that's exactly what my sister did." But rather than responding "Oh, all right then. I guess it makes sense," the reader says, "I believe that she did it in real life, but in this story I wasn't convinced."

Fiction, particularly realist fiction, is eternally chained to the problem of plausibility. Very little trumpets an author's failure as clearly as the words, "It didn't seem believable to me." And the first challenge of writing from real life is recognizing that the fact that events actually took place may make the story *less* plausible—if only because the author has failed to worry about whether or not it is. What we accept without question from everyday life must be proved in fiction.

And there are challenges to "real stories" beyond plausibility. "That would make a great story for you to write!" people often tell me when I recount some odd occurrence, an extraordinary coincidence, or maybe eccentric behavior I've observed. But my experience is that those amusing tales are almost always a complete failure as fiction.

Let's say I'm at a dinner party and I tell the story of the night the police came to my childhood home thinking we had a prowler—because my father, training to hike the Appalachian Trail, had taken to sleeping in our back yard. The reactions to that story are likely to be along the lines of "Wow!" and "That's hilarious." Maybe, "You had a wild upbringing, didn't you?" And of course, "You should write a story about that." And those are perfectly fine responses to an anecdote, but missing is any sense of a deeper meaning, or of universality, a resonance beyond the facts and superficial impact of the episode.

That, for me, is the greatest challenge of crafting fiction from these sorts of real life events—unless I'm willing to change the narrative drastically. As a teacher told me many years ago, anecdotes and stories are not the same thing. I would add, they aren't even on a continuum. A story is not an anecdote that has been beefed up—it's a completely different form, with different goals. An anecdote is generally told to provoke a social response—laughter, amazement, surprise. With a story however, while the author may welcome those responses along the way, they are unlikely to be the ultimate goal. An anecdote seeks as its end what a story may use as its means.

We are all looking for ideas, many of us in a state of perpetual if low-level anxiety over whether we are out of them. Stories that seem to present themselves as already developed, the next thing to already written, are a gift—though perhaps of the Trojan Horse kind. Initially, there is joy behind the thought, "Wow! That would make an amazing story!" But then, something like grief over the realization that what first appeared to be a kind of *gimme* is no easier to execute than any other work, no less subject to revision, no closer to taking the shape and form of a piece of literature than is any story that our imaginations construct. And in fact, the "truth" of the story may be making things more difficult.

Like so many writers, I have felt bereft when a story I thought would be a straightforward project turns into another quagmire, another mess, another adventure in hoping and doubting and trying and failing and maybe ultimately succeeding—but who knows? Maybe never succeeding. And that is all the more difficult when I am haunted by an already existing version of the story, the events as they occurred.

I don't try to make real life events into fiction anymore, but I'm not arguing against fictionalizing real events—not for other people. I am only suggesting that once a true story has been thrown into the fictional world it has no more power than does any original concept; yet it seems to. It should be just as subject to revision, just as concerned with plausibility; yet it resists that. It must be just as concerned with gravitas, about its reason to exist as any other story; but it argues throughout for its right to remain as it is. A "true" story has a certain kind of intelligence, a wily, unhelpful ability to argue its own case.

An infinite number of alternate realities.

Impossible to comprehend when existential theories are in play, well worth the effort when crafting stories is your goal.

The Success Gap

I KNOW PRECIOUS FEW writers who don't keep a mental inventory of how their own accomplishments and disappointments compare to those of their friends. That isn't because writers are inherently petty or ungenerous. Noticing successes one hasn't had is next to inevitable in a career with no logical professional pathway to success, no common measure of success, and no agreement about what constitutes success. The whole subject is so chaotic, so random, keeping score can sometimes seem like the only ordering principle available—even as one rails about the unfairness of the tally that it shows.

I personally know a dozen or more authors who seem to me to deserve a kind of success and fame that has eluded them. Sometimes their disappointments are attributable to the fashions of literature at the time. Sometimes, it seems as though they haven't been well-marketed. But often, I have no idea why a certain book or author doesn't catch fire when their work seems to me to be so superior to so much of what does.

And then there are the inexplicable hits.

Whatever the rhyme, reason, or lack of either to career rewards, these discrepancies can lead to social landmines. I have made some stunning mistakes by bragging to friends about having reached goals that are not yet within sight for them. In my defense, it didn't *feel* like bragging at the time. It felt more like expressing my own disbelief at my own good fortune, like using friends to confirm for me that these wonderful things had truly happened. It felt like exuberance. But looking back now, I can see that on these occasions I was at best insensitive and at worst a bit of a jerk. That phrase "using friends"— that's pretty much the crux of the problem right there. Friends don't use friends—especially to make themselves feel even better about grasping a brass ring that the friend has barely glimpsed.

And, on the other side, I have spent days, sometimes weeks, in the doldrums over achievements I have yet to achieve—or may well never achieve. I have taken breaks from Facebook because it has seemed to exist for the purpose of making me feel bad about my career. I have smiled through genuine sorrow while congratulating a friend.

This is a complicated subject—and a touchy one. In the past when I've written about my efforts to handle jealousy and comparison and self-doubt, I've heard from people taking me to task for my pitiable if not contemptible inability to rise above such pettiness. These communications often include the claim: "*I'm* not jealous of my friends. *I'm* happy for them."

It's a claim to which I have two reactions: The first is, "How lovely, and how lucky for you." The second is, "I am often envious of friends and I am also happy for them." It is a mistake to believe that envy precludes a generous response. In my experience, envy rarely has much at all to do with what one wishes for one's friend or colleague, and everything to do with one's own doubts and anxieties about oneself. Maybe envy isn't even the best word for the stomach-churning one can feel at a friend's good news. Maybe the better word is *fear*.

Most of us can handle a little jealousy now and then. What threatens us far more powerfully is the notion that the gods of who deserves to write have spoken, and they haven't had much good to say about us.

A common exhortation is, "That's why you have to make it about the work" and I've been guilty of saying this myself, in irritatingly pious tones. It's taken me a while to understand why this prescription is very close to a *non sequitur*. When a lawyer is disappointed at not making partner, we don't say, "You can't get hung up on that stuff. You have to make it about the work." Ditto, when a professor is denied tenure, or when a pre-med doesn't get into med school, and so on. Having goals and being anxious about meeting them, or disappointed when they go unmet, feeling hurt by a lack of recognition, none of this means that one's commitment to the quality and importance of one's work is somehow shaky. Ambition for success and a passion for excellence are not in conflict. It seems unjust to take a perfectly natural response like envy—or fear—and imply that it indicates a lack of seriousness about one's work.

We don't say to bummed out football players who have just lost the Super Bowl, "That's why it has to be all about the work." We say, "That really sucks."

Maybe the advice to "make it about the work" is so common because it hints at a path around envy. But I'm not convinced there is such a path. There are only coping mechanisms—and also kindnesses.

Some time ago, a colleague who had just won a big award asked me why so few people he knew were bringing it up and congratulating him. Maybe because it wasn't my ego seeking the strokes, it was easy for me to understand then that it's not the job of the people who are struggling to go out of their way to celebrate the successes of those who have surged ahead. It is, if anything, the responsibility of the surging one to take time to show genuine interest in what's happening with those who are struggling still, and to give them encouragement.

I say this as someone who, like many writers, exists in both roles. I have had some wonderful unanticipated "triumphs" and I have had my share of frustrations, too. For people who can't get books accepted or have never been nominated for an award, my career may well look enviable. For people who have won tons of awards and sold hundreds of thousands of books, my career doubtless looks modest. But, most importantly—and I freely admit I don't always achieve this—I need to be aware of my audience when I whine about what I haven't accomplished, and when I brag about what I have.

There is of course something serious and unfixable underlying all of this: the chaotic fuckedupedness of the profession itself. The elements that go into success of any kind are strange, unpredictable, not always related to quality—a concept over which there is never anything resembling consensus, nor should there be. Working hard is certainly a good plan, but it guarantees nothing. Having talent sounds promising—if only anyone knew what that meant. Social connections to powerful people, even just the power-monger-of-the-month, can play a too evident role in recognition. One's ethnic identity, one's gender, one's sexual orientation, one's economic status, one's social habits, one's appearance, one's city of residence, one's age, one's luck, one's luck, one's luck... those and a million more factors all interact and influence outcomes. There is simply no way to control this thing.

We are murky beings, we humans, and this for sure is a murky career. I have given up on expecting perfect sensitivity from anyone, or perfect generosity of spirit. I have stopped thinking ill of people who occasionally lapse in handling either success or frustration well.

And as for those who consistently don't, I avoid them when I can. Not everything about being a writer is unclear, it turns out.

The Literary Birds & Bees:
How One Novel Was Conceived

NOVELS DIFFER FROM HUMAN beings in that we can't know much about how they, as a species, are conceived. There is no single narrative for spawning a narrative. No literary sperm and ovum prerequisites necessary—that we know of, anyway. And while stories of how novels are conceived likely lack the titillation potential of stories about how babies are made, I am always interested in hearing them.

My own tale begins with an abandonment. Mid-2009. A twice drafted novel, already sold while in progress, as part of a two-book deal. My dawning realization that it wasn't very good. My fighting that realization. *But I got going at this writing game too late to waste years on a practice book*, I told myself. The Heavens laughed. And so I found myself beginning again—and again, and again.

For years. I woke up ill with anxiety, doubting I could complete the task. I became certain that I'd already said what I had to say in my ten stories, that I was finished writing fiction. The well was dry. The need to communicate, sated. And the novel was a dumb form anyway. (This, mumbled while pouting and kicking at the couch. *Stupid novels.*)

By January 2012, when I arrived at an annual retreat with seven other women, I was a wreck. It had been nearly three years since I'd withdrawn my mediocre novel, and in that time, I had started and stopped at least four new projects. I hated them. They hated me. I hated myself. Not every aspect of myself (I'm a shockingly good cook), but enough to tip the balance that way. Oh, and did I mention I had given up? Well, not officially. I hadn't yet informed my agent or my editors, but deep in my heart I just knew…

And so on the first night of that retreat, I told my dear friends, all writers too, that the project was doomed, so I thought I would just use the week to goof off, reading and writing what*ever*—prose poems, limericks, ad copy—rather than keep trying to make a book appear from thin, unimaginably ungenerous air.

I spent the first five days there reading Ovid on my iPad. Specifically, I read about Medusa and I read about Pygmalion and Galatea. I read about the woman who could turn people into stone and the woman who had once been stone herself. I imagined Medusa seeking out Galatea so she could ask for a report on what it was like to be a statue—Galatea being the only person who could inform her about that state. *So, about these people I keep petrifying, what are they going through?* I felt sorry for Medusa, for her hideous visage, for her shitty future, for how everyone hated her. And I felt sorry for Galatea, too, awakening from eternity to find herself being fondled by some man whose appreciation of her perceived perfection left no room for her choice.

And Rodin! I looked up Rodin's sculptures of Galatea and wondered whether while he sculpted her—a sculpture of a human who had been a sculpture—it ever occurred to him that she might awaken one day…I even wrote a six word story about that:

"Rodin Sculpting Galatea"

It is impossible not to hope.

And then on day six of the retreat I wrote 5,000 words of the novel that would be published the following spring. 5,000 words that remained essentially the same through every revision. And the next day, I wrote the next 4,000 words, words also still present in the book.

I tell the story that way, with no real lead up to that happy turn because that is what it felt like at the time. One day I couldn't write a novel and would never be able to, and the next day I could write a novel—a novel that over the following year poured out of me in a way no story ever has, in a way I doubt any future novel ever will. Poured out of me as though all I'd had to do was remove the lid and tip the container just a bit.

But what had actually happened?

It is, of course, impossible to know. Creativity cannot be understood. It can be analyzed and maybe even quantified in some ways, but never understood. I can point to many elements as having likely helped. Wise comments from the women there with me, and also from other friends who were not. A sudden realization that having cut my teeth writing about families, I was tired of writing about families. My therapist's observation that the goal of writing to fulfill a contract might be a realistic one, but was probably not a very creatively inspiring one, so perhaps I might want to have a different goal—like writing a really good book. But among those many elements and more, it is the five days of reading Ovid to which I now return.

This is my understanding: I needed to relocate my obsessions, to find them somewhere other than in my own head. The novel, *Life Drawing*, is about many things, including the relationships between art and mortality, art and grief, art and redemption. What does it mean, as an artist, to *give life* to human figures? What are the emotions behind that impulse? What does it mean when an artist cannot *give life*? And how does all of that relate to the human capacity, again and again, to renew our faith in others, in ourselves? As I write those questions now, they sound reductive to me. I want to say, "Of course, the novel is about *much* more than that..." And it is—I hope, and I believe. But those are three of the strands I have braided at its heart: Mortality, forgiveness, and art.

So, when did I figure out that all this reading about stone figures, mortal petrification, statues coming to life, and irreversible punishment had any bearing on the book that I wrote? It was the day on which the manuscript was taken from my hands and sent off to the copyediting department to be cleaned up. Only then could I see those five days of reading Ovid as something other than just a necessary breather, and more like an uncanny, unconscious intuition for how to relocate my deepest, troubled, hopeful self. Not the self that is concerned with book contracts. But the self that makes me to want to write.

And that is how novels are made.

Except it is not.

The next novelist to tell you the conception story of her book is unlikely to recount immersing herself in Ovid's *Metamorphosis* for five days. She may talk about the bad marriage it was necessary she end. Or writing longhand. Or traveling for research. Or doing yoga. Or she may stare blankly at the suggestion that writing a novel requires anything more than a disciplined six hours a day at her desk. All of these are important stories to hear—as I hope this one is, too. If only so that when you are stuck—if you ever *are* stuck—you will know that there is no one way to make a book. And you will know too that, as we stumble through this work, we are sometimes both intuitive and blind in helpful, uncontrollable ways.

Or, to tell this story a little differently, when I was on retreat in January of 2012, I thought I might write something about Galatea and Medusa, but I started to write my novel instead. And on the day that I finished it—only then—I realized that I had done both.

In Defense of Adverbs, Guardians of the Human Condition

I WANT PEOPLE TO love adverbs. More than that, I want them to believe, as I do, that adverbs are the part of speech that best captures the human condition.

But first, let's review what we've all been told: Adverbs are bad. Adverbs should be excised from our prose. I love this advice, not because it's right (it's wrong) but because of how ludicrous the idea is that a part of speech could be *bad*. What are the odds? I'm no expert in the development of languages, but this seems like a bizarre notion to me. Like saying, *pronouns are silly.* Or, *verbs are so annoying.* Presumably adverbs exist for a legitimate purpose, evolved to fulfill a communicative need—or they wouldn't exist.

So why this bad rap? My theory is that it's not because we overuse adverbs, but because we have lost the sense of their actual potential and purpose. Language does indeed evolve, and for stodgy people like me who are attached to the grammar they were taught when young, it can seem to devolve.

As often used, adverbs *are* expendable. In the sentence, "She shouted loudly," the adverb adds nothing—which is commonly the complaint, the advice often something like: "Your verb can do the work. You don't need the extra word." And here, your verb is doing the work—if the work is only to communicate the volume at which this person spoke. The meaning of "she shouted loudly" is essentially identical to the meaning of "she shouted."

But adverbs are modifiers—not handy tools for reiteration. To modify means to *change, alter, amend.* Adverbs modify the part of speech to which they are subordinate. In other words, they are not unnecessary emphasizers as in the previous example. They don't exist to pad our writings with redundancy but to shade and even alter the verb's meaning in a particular sentence. *She shouted reluctantly.* She shouted, predictably. *She shouted unceasingly.* She shouted hopelessly. *She shouted victoriously.* She shouted wistfully—somehow, despite the power of her voice.

Which of these adverbs is unnecessary? Which merely compounds the meaning of the verb? These sentences may not be brilliant, but they are not "flabby" as so many claim that sentences with adverbs are doomed to be. Not a one of them could be replaced with the sentence, "She shouted" and still mean the same thing. And that is a useful test of an adverb's worth: would the verb (or adjective) it modifies be essentially identical without the adverb? If so, then the conclusion should not be that adverbs are bad, but that the writer is bad at using them. (How strange that when writers fail in other ways, we blame them and not the instrument of their failure. When people write bad dialogue, we don't declare that all dialogue is bad…)

At their most evocative, adverbs provide something like the opportunity that metaphors do, though in a less elaborate, less overt way. Metaphors, to be more than a bit reductive, "work" not because the two things being compared are identical, but because they share some characteristics, and, just as importantly, *do not* share others. "Her glove, multicolored, its fingers barely spread, could have been some exotic bird about to take flight." There's just enough there—the many colors, the fingers reminiscent of feathers—to make the introduction of the notion of flight, *via* the comparison to a bird, seem natural. But what makes the notion revelatory is that gloves do not fly. A simple description of the glove, "The glove was multi-colored and its fingers were somewhat spread," also tells you what the glove looks like, but doesn't modify its essential gloveness with any other notions—notions of flight in this case.

"She shouted wistfully" is not a metaphor, but it functions in similar ways. Wistfulness does not contradict the fact of shouting, but introduces an element, a tone, that is not inherent to shouting. It changes the essential shoutingness of the shout, in a way that the word "loudly" does not.

Adverbs, because they alter the presumed or "regular" meaning of another word, are uniquely suited to bringing freshness to our language, and to shaking us up. They are unsettling in all the best ways. We think we know how people shout: loudly. We hear the word "shout," and that is the one thing we know. But we also learn a new way that a shout might emerge; and adverbs shoulder the task of surprising us with that.

I learned pretty much everything I know about adverbs reading Nabokov. Nabokov not only uses adverbs freely, he uses tricks to get the most out of them. He very often places the adverb—or adverbs—before the verb, so as you read, you have the modifier which supplies the mood, the atmosphere, the manner of an action, and *then* you have the action. From *Pnin*: "Untenderly she cradled the receiver."

This reversal creates a suspense composed of ignorance and curiosity both. The reader is engaged, active in the sentence, at least in part because of an awareness that she doesn't know how it will be resolved. While it's true that one often doesn't know how a sentence will be resolved, Nabokov's manipulation of the modifier, deploying it ahead of that which it modifies, brings the mystery of the sentence into high relief.

And the adverb, rather than being an afterthought, swallowed by dominance of the verb and its power to determine event, sets the tone so the verb never exists in its most usual form, later to be changed or modified. When the action occurs, we already know in what manner it does so, making the verb itself both more eloquent and less of a bully. That's not an effect that every sentence requires or from which they would all even benefit, but it's a tool, a trick well worth trying.

Similarly, while it might grow tiresome to read sentence after sentence containing contradictions of the sort found between "untenderly" and "cradled," there's a lot to be said for exploring the use of such internal tensions in a single description.

Nabokov frequently piles adverbs on, long strings of them, introducing into the sentence something like the effect of a collage.

Again, from *Pnin*: "Nowadays, at fifty-two, he was crazy about sun-bathing, wore sport shirts and slacks, and when crossing his legs would carefully, deliberately, brazenly display a tremendous stretch of bare shin." The adverbs not only modify the verb, they modify one another, doing a lot of work along the way. Before the reader even knows what verb is to come, the adverbs have painted a portrait of the character—while somehow also mocking him. And in fact, though the verb "displays" matters to the sentence, completing the picture, it seems to be subservient to the adverbs there, rather than the other way around.

Nabokov also uses adverbs for more than their descriptive powers: He harnesses their sound. Also from *Pnin*: "Gravely, comfortably, the gray-headed conductor sank into the opposite seat..." That interlocking alliteration, that chugging rhythm, it all evokes the turn and lull of train wheels.

That's an awful lot for a part of speech to do. Especially a bad part of speech.

Which brings me to the human condition, mysterious, ambiguous, in flux. This is not a state best represented by verbs, with their defining decisiveness; nor adjectives, like darts, pinpointing specific qualities. Nor is human life a noun—not as lived. Conjunctions don't quite do it either. Articles, obviously not. But adverbs! With their dedicated, infinite flexibility, their ability to speak among themselves, to disagree yet never negate, to surprise; to hold one's attention with their resistance to what is assumed, with their beauty. Is it too fanciful to say that life itself is an adverb, the modification of those two inevitable verbs—to be born, to die?

Perhaps it is. That may be a stretch. But this is the glory of language, after all. That it allows for these stretches, these leaps, some profound, others less so. But all of them results of our attempts to communicate, to understand, to understand more, to communicate more fully. And there is no part of speech better able to assist than that much maligned, underworked, ugly duckling: the adverb. Humbly, eloquently, sneakily, daintily, elegantly. Yes. All of that, and more.

Line Edits II

HER DATE WAS BORING.

Her date was spectacularly boring.

The Subject is Subjectivity

I HAD BEEN WRITING off and on for many years, been through endless (some feeling literally endless) workshop experiences, and had an MFA before I understood that taste in literature is subjective. I mean, I knew that, in some way—but not in any particularly helpful way. The realization came at the second meeting of the first writing course I ever taught. I was in the middle of a discussion of Grace Paley's story "Conversations With My Father," a story I love, a story it never occurred to me anyone else wouldn't love (a story that in my heart of hearts I still believe everyone should love) and it became clear to me that not everyone in the room loved it.

"How many of you liked this story?" I asked. Two-thirds of the hands went up.

I resisted the impulse to argue with the remaining third, and asked a series of simple questions instead. How many people liked Faulkner? A third or so. How many liked Woolf? Around half.

"I hope you'll all remember this when your work is being workshopped," I said. "If half the folks in here think you're on the right track, you're even with Virginia Woolf and ahead of William Faulkner."

Soon after that night, an editor with whom I had worked several times rejected a story of mine—in no uncertain terms. She was kind, but there was none of that "oh, this was close" stuff. It was an unambiguous no, and it hit me hard. I fell into one of those *I probably shouldn't even try to be a writer* patches, until, a week later, another editor called me up, whispering in shaky, anxious tones that he had just read the same story and was hoping, hoping (hoping!) that it was still available for publication.

"Why yes, I believe it is."

I allowed myself a certain sense of vindication as I hung up the phone, but what I eventually faced is that neither of them was right. The accepting editor wasn't a winning argument against the rejecting one. As much as it can be tempting to believe otherwise, the illusion of objectivity in response to art is an illusion indeed. For better and worse, when you decide to write, you hurl yourself and your cherished work product into a world ruled by individual taste. The only way in which either editor was right is that both were right. The story was wrong for the first journal and a good fit for the second—but not for any reason beyond their subjective responses to the piece. Writing is not a fixed currency.

There are always more ways to learn this lesson. In 2007 an essay of mine appeared in the book *The Best Creative Nonfiction, Volume I*. The anthology was published by Norton, the selection made by the editors of *Creative Nonfiction* magazine. I was thrilled to have the piece included—and I was also amused, because a couple of years before, *Creative Nonfiction* magazine had rejected the same piece. A sad little D-list Xeroxed rejection slip. And again, that isn't a matter of self-correction on their part. It's almost certainly a question of whose desk it crossed the first time, and whose desk it crossed the second time. No one right; no one wrong.

Am I saying there's no such thing as bad writing or good writing? I am saying that long, long before the question of inherent quality can be addressed, the dominance of subjective response has so trampled the conceit that it's a question barely worth asking. And it's a question I particularly dislike because in the asking lies the implication that some of us are more entitled to write than others, because some of us are "good" and others of us are "bad." I would far rather err in the direction of inclusion than risk endorsing that scheme.

Much of this, the simple fact of subjective responses, should be obvious. It should be a fact we carry in our heads at all times. But it is difficult, if illogically so, for many of us to remember, as the rejections pile up, that each one is only the subjective response of an individual reader and not a judgment from on high about the worth of that piece or about our right to write. Whatever we know to be true, some of us cannot move past the fantasy that if we are just good enough, then everyone will love our work—a fantasy with a pretty tough downside since it follows that if not everyone loves our work, we must not be good enough.

Over the course of many years, during more and less successful attempts to start writing again, I would join writing workshops—some teacher-led, some not. There were a lot of valuable aspects to those experiences, even the ones that were brief, but there were also downsides, some of which speak directly to the subject of subjectivity.

I observed—and sometimes participated in—a pull toward reaching a consensus about both the quality of the presented work and what steps the author might take in revision. This may grow out of a desire to offer the author a clear perspective and clear plan, but, laudable a desire as that may be, agreement among eight or ten readers is unlikely to reflect accurately what each individual feels. Those colleagues who might have uniquely helpful suggestions, perhaps ones that can't be so easily absorbed into group advice, may go unheard. In workshop settings, it's crucial that authors locate those participants who will be their best readers—and if everyone's voice is blended into one, that can't take place.

Of course there are workshops that do the opposite, workshops where the variety of reactions is dizzying, subjectivity on full display, every voice, every opinion given equal time. This too is problematic, because not all readers are created equal. There is a difference between one who sees room for improving your work, but likes the basic idea, and a reader who just hates what you are doing. The latter may be voluble, but is unlikely to offer much useful advice. (Had I asked the editor who rejected my story for help improving it, I can't imagine what she could have told me. She so disliked the premise of the thing. Really, she could only have said what she did say: "I'd like to see something different.")

In my experience, workshops rarely make those distinctions, rarely suggest that people who thoroughly dislike a piece might want to hold their counsel, allowing the people who support the author's intent to do most of the talking. But doing so might not only max out the chances that the writer will receive productive advice. It might also normalize the fact that there are always likely to be people who don't connect to any given work, that detractors are not a sign of anything—except that you have written a piece and shown it to enough people to provoke a typical range of responses.

It doesn't get any easier to welcome subjective responses to one's work with book publication, in part because of the love-fest that precedes a book's launch. Before my collection of stories came out, I spent eighteen months in a lovely bubble in which resided my editors (who love my book), my agent (who loves my book), my publicist (who loves my book), my husband (who loves my book), and so on. With publication, the bubble burst. Suddenly I heard from reviewers and readers who didn't know me from a hole in the wall, people with absolutely no interest in reassuring me—or themselves—that my work is great.

It is painful when those first negative comments roll in. There are ways to soothe yourself—like comparing notes with other authors; like drafting letters of protest that you never send. I went online and read bad reviews of classic books. *Okay, there are people who hate Dickens too. And Jane Austen! And* Goodnight Moon*!! Subjectivity applies to us all!* I can't pretend my euphoria lasted long, but it bought me a few good moments.

Subjectivity isn't only important though because its prevalence means that you have opportunities to learn how to take criticism in stride. There is one huge benefit to knowing that you can't please all of the people any of the time: You might as well stop trying. And what liberation there is in that! A writer's job, it turns out, is to write what she believes is her best work, and then hope that it will find the readers to whom it speaks; not to try to write the first book in the history of the world that everybody loves. And what wonderful news that is!

Of course, like my joy at Jane Austen's critical pans, that is a state of mental purity difficult to maintain. But I have a mantra now for when I catch myself longing for universal adoration: Fifty percent gets you to Virginia Woolf.

Tales of Sorrow, Tales of Woe

THE STORY IS ABOUT loss. For me, it seems, the story is often about loss. In the stories in my first book there are at least a half-dozen deaths and some comparable number of physical ailments, chronic conditions, and disabilities. My novel, too, begins with the disclosure of a loss and then moves into the worlds of infertility and dementia. And though I may be an extreme case, I'm hardly alone in my choice of saddening subject matter.

Many writers gravitate toward the depiction of tragic events. It's almost *de rigueur* in a writing class that there will be a hefty helping of cancer tales and a smattering—at least—of fatal car accidents. Equally inevitable: There will be people who feel that those subjects have been, well, done to death. Tales of sorrow can be a tough sell—literally. I once attended a panel discussion at which an editor of a prestigious magazine asked, in tones of great contempt: "Do we *really* need another story about somebody's sister dying of cancer?"

My first response was pure irritation, fueled by my realization that I shouldn't bother knocking on that editor's door with my wares. My second response, less wholly self-involved, was that while I understood exhaustion with the subject matter, I didn't agree that the subject matter was itself exhausted. Undoubtedly, there can be a certain sameness to these tales of loss, not to mention a whiny quality. Undoubtedly some such stories run together, indistinct and unoriginal. But they don't have to. The challenges that arise with depictions of sorrow are not insurmountable.

Though they are challenges indeed. It is a well-known peculiarity of fiction that the more overtly a reader is *asked* to sympathize with a character, the less likely she is to do so. It's also true that for many of us the impulse to write about loss grows from experiencing sorrow ourselves, which can make it difficult for us to see that grieving character as anything but wholly sympathetic. These two facts in combination do not bode well for success. After all, nobody, not even the kindest-hearted of readers, wants to be a guest at someone else's pity party.

But, as I said, there are ways to increase your odds of not driving readers away. For starters, it is helpful if the sorrowing hero isn't too much of a saint. Just because a character views herself as a victim, a wronged angel, lacking any responsibility or flaws, doesn't mean the story has to echo that view. Though if the incidents resonate with events of the author's life, it can be challenging to gain the kind of distance that allows for complicating a portrait of suffering saintliness. Challenging, but again, not impossible. Giving the character hobbies and habits, interests and inclinations very different from the author's own can be almost magically useful. If the author has never gardened and her character is an avid gardener, that fact alone will require that her imagination get to work, and will force her into fictionalizing both character and situation more completely.

Another approach to keeping your reader from feeling overly tasked to provide unending sympathy is to use a secondary character to challenge the central character in some way. This is particularly helpful with a story which is—as many loss stories are—about someone who cannot get past her grief. That's a very human problem, and one worthy of fictional exploration; but it's also a set-up for having your reader throw the story across the room with an exasperated "Oh, get over it!"

One of the best edits I ever received addressed exactly this. I'd written a story about a young widow, my narrator, whose central problem was that three years after her husband's death she showed no signs of moving forward. She was the classic stuck character, and though I found her entirely sympathetic, maybe too sympathetic, I couldn't deny that other people found her frustrating—in a way that seeped into their finding the story itself frustrating.

My editor suggested that I have my character's best friend, whom she habitually pushed around while demanding his sympathy, articulate every frustration a reader might feel. That scene, that expression of anger, was like a rush of fresh air in the piece, breaking the sealed quality that had resulted from the narrator's previously unchallenged, inactive self-pity. And as a side note, I had no trouble writing that scene, discovering along the way that though I had thought I found my character only sympathetic, that wasn't entirely true.

(This is a technique with broader use than only within stories about loss. There are many times when having a supporting player, or even the central character, express a frustration that the reader likely feels will help diffuse the reader's irritation.)

Another approach to the timeworn subject of loss is to try to defamiliarize stories that might sound, in summary, like a million others that have come before. The aforementioned dismissive editor doesn't think the world needs another story about "somebody's sister dying of cancer" because he thinks he already knows what that story will be. But he can be proved wrong. A.S. Byatt's brilliant story "A Stone Woman" depicts a daughter whose grief over her mother's death leads to literal petrification. Mother dying? Old hat for us literary types. Daughter crystalizing? Not so much.

And one needn't become a fabulist to make an old problem seem new. Another approach is to look to structure for a fresh perspective, employing ordering principles beyond that of linear chronology. Collage, for example, requires a type of intellectual engagement that a more linear structure may not, just by virtue of requiring a kind of puzzling-through. When the story asks for a response like that, beyond and distinct from sympathy, the reader is likely to feel less bombarded by those more emotional demands.

An intertwining, secondary plot line contrasting and resonating with the central one can also offer counterpoint to the potential drag and familiarity of stories of loss. A mother dies and her son can't get over it. Sounds familiar. A mother dies and her son who has been set since childhood on breaking the world's record for eating chicken wings and is in training to do just that, can't get over it…This example may (or may not?) be a stretch, but it would be difficult to read that tale of loss and think that you had read it a thousand times before.

It is possible to make any old subject new. To say otherwise is to deny centuries if not millennia of retold tales. And with the subject of loss, there are some remarkable rewards. Prominent on my desk is a note I received from a woman who recently read my story about that widow stuck in her grief. The woman who wrote me had also been widowed for several years, and my depiction of stuckness, as well as the challenge to it that my narrator's best friend articulates, set her thinking about her own difficulty moving forward.

To be clear, the story did not change her life. She wasn't immediately relieved of her grief, nor shown an easy way through it. But by providing something like a mirror, the story illuminated something she had been unable to see; and as long as grief stories can do that for someone in pain, I will keep writing them—and I hope that others will as well.

Do we really need another story about someone's sister dying of cancer? Yes. Don't be ridiculous. Of course we do.

House Lessons III:
Showing Not Telling

AFTER EIGHTEEN YEARS, WE were ready to move, my husband and I, selling the home in which we raised our three children, the home in which we unimaginably slipped from being young to being members of AARP, from having four parents to having two, from believing we would raise four children, to grieving the one who was stillborn. It is the home in which I made birthday cakes decorated as maps of family vacations, and designed Halloween costumes to do Martha Stewart proud, the home in which we all punched down the Rosh Hashanah challah dough each year because I, the nonbeliever, believed this was a way for us to pray. It is the home in which I grew panicky as my youngest child failed to crawl, month after month, the home in which I learned the meaning of words like *hypotonic* and *dyspraxia*. It is the home in which my husband and I have both lived the longest in our lives, a home in which I've heard almost all of my local writer friends read from their work, at one or another of our "salons." And it is—we believe—a work of art, an eighteen-year-long collaboration between us, two very different people who share a quirky sensibility and a desire to have a home unlike any other. And so, no two knobs on our kitchen cabinets match, and the walls are dotted with hanging, miniature chairs. And then there is the mess. This is the home in which I have waged an eighteen-year battle against my own inability to keep a house clean or anything close, the home in which I have unhappily faced the certainty that my chaos sometimes embarrasses my children in front of their friends.

We have lived novel after novel in this home.

But the experts are agreed that when you put your house on the market you are meant to erase yourself. House sales are all about competing narratives. My story, our story, was embedded in every room. The task for me was to render the house a blank page so a potential buyer could imagine writing, living, *her* story here.

No family pictures, my realtor said. *And nothing too idiosyncratic.*

Staging is the word the realtors use—a word that connotes both artificiality and a locus for unfolding events. And so I went from room to room removing objects that are, I realize, exactly the sort of telling details I might want in a piece of fiction. There was a mirror in our hall, bright red, with strange, multi-colored birds seemingly flying into it, that had to be replaced by another mirror, one with a simple light wood frame. On the inside of our powder room door an aluminum sign read: *Please flush after each use except when train is in the station.* That too has to go, the four screw holes filled, sanded, painted over. And the bright pink woodwork in our oldest daughter's room was deemed too gender specific, the chalkboard wall in our son's too young. The plumbing pipes that ran and turned just overhead in the basement and that I had painted the colors of the London tube map, were to be restored to their original black.

I was once asked in an interview why houses play so prominent a role in my work, and I gave a few answers, but the one on my mind as I prepared our house for sale had to do with how homes reveal character.

When I first started writing, I struggled with physical descriptions. Someone in a workshop once told me that a story of mine was "like two enormous brains arguing with each other under water or maybe in outer space." I now think that might make for an interesting work, but it wasn't my intent at the time; and so at some point around then, I decided to start placing my people in actual rooms. At first it was difficult for me—my interests were so entirely rooted in people's emotional interiors. Objects, floors, colors all seemed irrelevant. And so my early attempts at writing physical descriptions read as though I were ticking off a list: Okay, I mentioned the wall color; I talked about the age of the house; I described what everyone's wearing. Can I get on with it now?

I didn't understand the possible role of the physical world in fiction, at all. I can theorize about that being related to my ADD—we of deficient attention are often unconcerned with our physical surroundings. Moreover, my ADD may have been the cause of my skipping over so many descriptive passages as I read. Anything over an inch long can be challenging for someone with poor powers of concentration—the sort of person who measures prose by the inch. But whatever the cause, it all seemed irrelevant to me and to my dissections of my characters' emotional lives.

Until I discovered that the interiors of homes and the interior lives of the people who occupy them are often not so very distinct. In a short story, the right description of that crazy bird mirror of mine might go a long way to define the woman who chose to hang it in her entryway. Our choices (those unmatched kitchen cabinet knobs…) speak volumes about us. A character who paints her walls in jewel tones and hangs vibrant floral curtains in every room is immediately distinct from the one whose home displays a minimalist aesthetic. Those descriptions are shorthand, packed with information it might be difficult to otherwise convey.

As are living conditions that have less to do with intent and more to do with aspects of ourselves beyond our control. My messy, chaotic home is a manifestation of a truth about me, whether I like to admit that or not. My unkempt lawn was as well—and was quickly mowed, landscaped, brought to order by the people who ultimately bought our home. Driving by, seeing that, seeing the gate they put up, detecting ways in which they decided to exert control, I immediately understood how very different from me they must be. That it saddened me is a testament to the power of physical detail.

When we bought the house in 1995, this theory of neutralizing houses in order to sell them hadn't become orthodoxy, a phenomenon I blame on HGTV and its like. I don't remember seeing a single home then that wasn't overflowing with personality and therefore with narrative. In fact, in our house, when we first saw it, there was a telltale massive dark stain on the living room's hardwood floor, just next to the fireplace. Urine. The previous owners had potty-trained their twin sons in that central spot. *That should be in a story*, I think now, though the stain is long gone—so eloquent, so evocative a stain. I imagine the harried parents, overwhelmed with two babies. I imagine their tacit, exhausted agreement never to discuss the fact that the most convenient way they've found to potty train their boys is resulting in such costly damage to one of the finest features of their home. Marriages are conspiracies and this was evidence of the nature of theirs.

As I scrubbed away the narrative in which we lived, I found my thoughts returning to when we had no idea what our story would be.

There's a videotape of me, pregnant with my youngest in the summer of 1995, out in the yard, barely able to keep a straight face as I describe to the camera, to the children, to the future, that the reason the front door of our new home doesn't face the street is that during the Mesozoic Era there was some kind of extraordinary earthquake event, and the house was violently shifted sideways.

Wait, I'm not sure I caught that, my husband's voice says. *Tell us again. How exactly was the house moved?*

*Well...*I begin, my hand resting on my rounded front, a mock serious expression on my face. *A very, very long time ago, this house...*

Giotto's Perfect Circle

THE STORY GOES LIKE this: Back in the early fourteenth century, the Pope needed a painter for an important project, so he sent a courier to Florence, that bastion of all things painterly, to collect submission pieces from the hottest artists of the day. When the courier asked Giotto for a painting to take back to Rome, Giotto took his brush and drew a perfect red circle in one elegant stroke, pronouncing that to be his entry. The courier—as legend would have it—suggested that this was some bullshit, but Giotto retorted that the Pope would understand what it meant about his level of giftedness. And the Pope, of course, did understand and gave the commission to Giotto—which, as an aside, is why this is a story. If he hadn't, I doubt we'd still be talking about that circle some seven hundred years later.

I first heard about Giotto's bold move and nearly unique skill when I was fifteen and was—remember, not all teenagers are alike—a little obsessed with fourteenth century Christian art. I'm not sure how much I actually knew about it (not much, I suspect) but, as with so many teenage obsessions, I had a lot of posters. And it almost goes without saying that after hearing about Giotto's circle, I spent the bulk of my math period doodling-time that year trying to draw a perfect circle freehand. I failed. (I also failed math, but that's another story.)

Flash forward thirty-seven or so years, and now, much like the Pope, whom I assure you I resemble in no other respects, I find myself judging competitions from time to time. And much like Giotto, with whom I at least share a creative bent, I find myself being judged in competitions, as well.

We writers love a good analogy.

Unfortunately, there isn't an exact one here. There is no abstracted single element that a writer might submit to prove overall excellence, even in a hypothetical competition with no rules about word count and such. Among other reasons, we lack objectivity in our art. We lack a compass with which one might trace the perfection of a sentence, the genius of a single word. Though I admit I enjoy thinking about that scene. The courier, seeking an official short story writer for the Pope, arrives at the garret of a writer who sneers, takes out his pen, and scribbles: *Unmoored.* The courier suggests that this doesn't fit the bill. "Actually, His Holiness was looking for something more like a story. Even flash fiction…" And the writer smiles—a bit smug. "He will understand. He will recognize my genius. It is a perfect word."

Cut to Pope rolling his eyes. "Please don't waste my time with this idiocy…"

Which leads to the obvious question. What are literary judges looking for anyway? First answer, given as one who submits to contests herself: I don't have a clue. Second answer, given as someone who judges contests from time to time: Giotto's story isn't entirely irrelevant to what I'm looking for.

What I look for has nothing to do with perfection though, nor with the mastery of a single skill, but the qualities of confidence, distinctiveness, and memorability are all critical—and first impressions too. Because if you don't hook me on Page One, I am unlikely to turn to Page Two. Novels, even short stories, don't get their full length to prove their worth. An author's first job is to make a reader want to turn the page—and the very first time that desire takes hold is the most important time.

But how? There is no one answer, but it isn't wholly a mystery either.

In real life, face-to-face, confidence can either impress or irritate. It wobbles eternally on the wall separating it from its evil twin, arrogance. I suspect that the courier who visited Giotto that day muttered some version of *cocky bastard* as he stepped back out onto the street. But in writing, in fiction, there is a necessary relaxation a reader must experience, a surrender to someone else's imagination and to their care—and to their authority. When I talk about the quality that hooks me into a piece I'm reading for a contest, I often say things like, "I could just tell that someone was *doing* something. Someone was in charge."

It's tempting to reduce that to: Go big, or go home. But the problem with that exhortation is that it can be misleading about what "big" is. Big, when it comes to story openings, is often taken to mean shocking, but "big" in this context, does not mean shocking, or eventful, or anything except having intent. Not just jotting words on a page. Not just getting things rolling. But getting things rolling with authority. Having a confident intelligence beam through.

Distinctiveness is another such characteristic. The Pope walks into his den and finds a dozen or more easels there. On each one is the face of Christ, or of Christ's beatific mother, or the cherubic smiles of smiling cherubs, and then, like some emissary from the mid-twentieth century, a red circle appears. Just that.

One of these things is not like the others.

Whatever else happened in that moment, for sure one piece in the room stood out. There's no way the Pope didn't ask what the deal was, no way his curiosity wasn't piqued. And even an attentive papal *what the fuck?* is better than a dismissive papal *same old, same old*—which goes for literary judges and magazine editors too.

But suggesting "difference" as a goal without some explanation is a dangerous thing to do. When I talk about difference or about being distinctive, I am emphatically *not* talking about jettisoning all familiar, time-honored subject matter. Distinctiveness, for me, isn't about the subject at all. It might be the language. It might be the structure. It might be that intangible: voice. But to get me to read past page one, a story needs to feel like something I have never read before.

Every time I've judged a contest, I read once, and then make an informal Finalist pile. Then I take a few days off. And very often a funny thing happens: I find myself remembering one story more than the others, almost as if it were in color, while the others fade to black and white. It just kind of pops. That doesn't mean I remember the plot or even how I felt at the end, but just that it's the one haunting me. And that is almost always the one I choose.

I don't know how to advise anyone on how to make their work memorable, but I will say that for me, anyway, it has absolutely nothing to do with surface perfections, well-turned sentences, expertly handled point of view. That's a kind of funny thing for me to say, because I work hard at those very elements. But I think that for those of us who aim for a kind of smooth, well-crafted product, there's a danger of losing sight of what's really going to knock a reader off her feet. I'm not saying that craft and memorability are in opposition, just that it can be easy to begin to put all your faith in a kind of proficiency of execution, as if that were the whole task, perhaps because as a writer, proficiency, as opposed to something more like spark, like magic, feels like something over which one can have some control.

It's possible though that being memorable has to do with something more like risk. As I said, here we are, seven centuries after the fact, telling the story of Giotto's unquestionably risky move. Would anyone ever cast a thought to that courier's visit had Giotto's response been to whip out a canvas of *The Annunciation*? No. Playing it safe, doing the expected, following the rules, these are not likely to penetrate anyone's consciousness with the kind of power that makes a thing unforgettable.

There are, of course, caveats. Giotto didn't just paint any old circle in order to be different from his peers. He painted *the* circle. A perfect circle. He backed up the risk with skill.

But another caveat, a caveat to that caveat: Perfection was Giotto's game. It isn't a writer's. There's no such thing as perfection in this pursuit. So the lesson isn't take risks if you can execute with perfection. The lesson is take risks—but be aware that risks alone do not great art make.

Though who knows, maybe sometimes they do. Maybe sometimes the risk *is* the art. Even while I want to give clear advice, I could easily go on and on with caveats and caveats to my caveats and so forth *ad infinitum.* Because that's how writing advice has to be: equivocal, balanced always by its opposite, absolutely not absolute.

But, with no caveats, I stand behind this modest assertion: There is value, if of an unquantifiable sort, to holding that moment of Giotto's bravado in your head from time to time as you write. The boldness of it, and the oddness too. The confidence. The lunacy. The riskiness, of course. The rudeness. The presumption.

And the success.

Line Edits III

THEIR FIRST MINUTES AT the inn are all about disappointment. Charlotte's disappointment.

Their first minutes at the inn are all about disappointment. Charlotte's disappointment; and Ethan's management of Charlotte's disappointment.

Their first minutes at the inn are all about disappointment. Charlotte's disappointment; and Ethan's management of Charlotte's disappointment, which she is doing her best to conceal.

Their first minutes at the inn are all about disappointment. Disappointment and the management of disappointment. Charlotte's disappointment; and Ethan's management of Charlotte's disappointment. She is doing her best to conceal it, he knows. She just isn't doing a very good job.

Their first minutes at the inn are all about disappointment. Disappointment and the management of disappointment. Charlotte's disappointment; and Ethan's management of Charlotte's disappointment. And Charlotte's management of her own disappointment too, to be fair. She is doing her best to conceal it, he knows. She just isn't doing a very good job.

Father Chronicles:
The Persistence of Demons

When I was a twenty year old undergrad, back in 1982, I had a dream, an actual sleeping dream, in which Leonard Woolf and Vanessa Bell escorted Virginia herself into my dorm room and announced that she was mine now, in my care. She was very delicate, they told me. Tending her wasn't an easy job, they said—while she only glanced downward from beneath the great rim of her hat. Being all of twenty years old, and thinking myself a writer, I took this to mean, not that I had best watch out lest I have a mental breakdown (which was true and might have been helpful advice at the time), but that I was to inherit the mantle of genius.

Within months of having that dream, I dropped out of school for a bit, moved back in with my parents, had the aforementioned mental breakdown, eventually became engaged to (later marrying) a man I barely knew, and stopped being serious about writing for the next twenty years.

Genius!

In my life it has been an ugly word. My father, gone fourteen years now, was a *bona fide* genius. He was the sort of genius for whom even the people who roll their eyes at the word *genius* make an exception. And the fact that he was also one of the unhappiest, most personally dysfunctional people I have ever known did little to protect me from the message he delivered, both explicitly and also in more poisonous, potent forms, that to be anything other than a genius—anything *less* than genius—was to be, well, at best, a little sad. Pitiable. Pathetic.

My knowledge of my father's private miseries did little to protect me from this view, but his death in combination with more therapy than I'll ever admit to diminished its power, which is part of why, at the age of thirty-nine, just about two decades after having the dream that amplified my misguided conviction that genius should be my goal, I was finally able to write.

And write I did, mostly short stories, but some essays too. None of which caused anyone to use the G-word, nor caused me to feel that they should, or even to long that they would. I felt, for the first time in my life, that I was doing something as well as I could, which was all that seemed to matter. I had frustrating days of course, but overall the writing made me happy. Happier than I had ever been. Maybe it was the deceptively unambitious-seeming nature of short forms that let me relax. Maybe it was the gusting exhilaration of finally stepping out from within the dark of my father's shadow and from under the weight of the tragic standards by which he measured his own lonely, unhappy success. Whatever the cause, I was productive and I was enjoying it.

A happy ending, yes?

Well, yes; and also, no.

Because then there was a novel. Unfinished. And often uncooperative. And just look at what a big thing it is—a novel. Look at how huge an impression it might make. How excellent a vehicle it could be for being declared a you-know-what…or, more realistically, how it will surely make it evident that one is not. And look at what sustained faith it requires. How difficult a task! What room for one's neuroses that massive task leaves, within those frustrating days and all those inevitable missteps…Look at what space is created for the demons to creep back in.

If it isn't to be a work of genius, it isn't worth writing, you know…

I found myself struggling again with that thought—as I realized that I was not in fact writing *Mrs. Dalloway*. Or *Ulysses*. Not reinventing the form. Not revolutionizing literature. I understood very well that my personal best was not Virginia Woolf's best—and never would be. At nineteen, at twenty, I dreamed it was. At nearly fifty, I knew better. And if I was to believe my poor father, that made this whole writing pursuit pretty pointless.

If it isn't to be a work of genius, it isn't worth writing, you know...

Ugly. As I said. But that was the message I was given, loud and clear. Quiet and clear. At every imaginable volume—and always clear.

Sometimes, when I have tried to explain the damage this viewpoint has done to me, the difficulties it newly caused while writing that new book, I have struggled to define the distinction between my father's blind drive for admiration on the one hand, and a healthy ambition for excellence on the other. The best way I have found to parse the two is to say that in my father's emotional landscape, doing one's best was only a meaningful goal if one's best was better than everyone else's best. The simple knowledge of having achieved a personal best would be a sorry consolation, at most.

If you think about it enough, that is one of the saddest possible ways to look at life. Certainly, one of the loneliest. And had you known my father, you could have traced that sorrow, that solitude in his every gesture, every glance.

It is difficult for me sometimes, this writing thing—as it is for us all, I know, in our different ways. I am haunted daily by that other idea, not my own, of what my goal should be. When it takes up my brain and crowds away my knowledge of what dangerous nonsense it is, it bullies my lyrical side into babbling doubt. I become a study in blockage, in self-sabotage. Never mind the questionable wisdom of taking life advice from one person whose misery I witnessed daily for almost forty years, and longing to follow in the footsteps of another who did, after all, walk into a river and drown herself. Demons are not creatures of logic. Demons are not geniuses. They don't need to be. They are just persistent as hell.

But if you think about *that*, there's the seed for optimism right there.

Because it turns out that persistence is a powerful thing. One of the most powerful allies any one of us has. Directed demonically, it can shut you down for decades at a time. But it can also be the engine that keeps you typing, that causes the clattering keys to drown out the voices that would have you stop. *Persist, persist.* Be more stubborn eve than your own demons. *Persist. Persist.* Not for any reason other than that you promised yourself you would. Just for long enough to get it all out on the page.

For my father, *bona fide* genius and eternally unhappy man, it took that kind of fortitude to face the business of living through every day. I would study the pain of it settling into his bones, beaming out from his light brown eyes. I would watch him scrap and cobble his broken self through many an hour, often ungraceful, sometimes unkind, occasionally memorably generous, startlingly empathic. But always in profound psychic pain.

Our stories are strange things, all of ours. And the logic through which our narratives unfold is often both obvious and paradoxical. Even as I battle the toxic standards of success that my father breathed into my dreams, I find myself grateful for his example of how fiercely one can try to fight a demon down.

Persist. Persist.

Empty Now

I AM EMPTY NOW. I have been empty for months. I have no stories inside me, none that are anxious or even willing to emerge. My imagination has taken on aspects of a phantom limb. Occasionally, I feel a twinge, but when I try to attend to it, I discover nothing there. Where dozens of short stories have jostled for space over the years, where hundreds of characters have lived, where my novel once resided, there is now a hollow space.

I think about this hollow a lot. Nature may abhor a vacuum, but, oddly, I don't hate this feeling of imaginative emptiness. I would describe my emotional stance toward it as something closer to a combination of respect and resignation. It wins. That's non-negotiable. I don't get to order my imagination to refill. I have to wait.

Some might call this writer's block, but I have always disliked the term—and not only because I don't know where, if anywhere, the apostrophe goes. I use the phrase sometimes, as a kind of shorthand, but the imagery is wrong for me, the metaphor fails. There isn't an impediment between me and the work I might produce. There is this hollow. This absence. This twinge that signifies nothing. The stories aren't being impeded. They don't exist.

The distinction matters to me. Emotionally. If I imagine myself blocked, it feels like a disorder of some kind. It worries me. But if I imagine that there is a chamber, always there, a space my imagination fills sometimes, and sometimes does not fill, it feels to me more like a process. Maybe even a natural process.

In fact, it feels strangely simple: I have used up my material, the stuff from which I craft stories. I don't have anything now. Maybe I will have more soon. Or not soon. Or not.

I don't like the thought of that last possibility, but of course it is a possibility. It is always a possibility. For every writer. On any given day. We always live with the specter of this hollow as eternal companion.

I attribute some of my current emptiness to having finished a novel recently. For so long, it filled all of me; of course it has left an emptiness behind. But I don't think that ending a consuming project is the only route to the state in which I find myself. Sometimes, my narrative-making ability is otherwise engaged, having nothing to do with writing fiction. My daughter who has special needs leads a life that doesn't follow any of the templates that exist for her older siblings— even allowing for variation. I am constantly spinning narratives in my mind about her and her future, crafting possible paths, writing alternate scenarios. Starting them and revising as circumstances change. I am making up her life with her as we go along—to a far greater degree than I might were her strengths and challenges otherwise. She is the great creative project of my life.

And—an easier realm for me—I am building an addition onto our new home. To design a space is to immerse yourself in narrative: Here is how we will live in it; this is the course of a day; this is the sort of area we will use for seeing friends; for doing work; for eating meals. These are the characters we must take into account.

I have also been traveling a lot, for work. I'm not naturally good at keeping track of logistics, so I have to tell myself the story of my own itinerary over and over, every trip, before I can conceptualize where I will be and how I will get there. Narrative, again.

I'm not saying that life has to stop in order for me to write. It never has stopped, and I've written plenty. I suppose I'm suggesting that it's inevitable that for many of us there will be periods when the generative, creative energies are otherwise engaged. That making up stories can't happen every day. That it's okay.

Though the fact is, we *do* make up stories all day long. All of us. To go to the grocery store is to spin a thousand tales. A thousand silent tales. About what you need to buy, why you need it, how you will use it.

About what you will do while you're there. How long it will be before you go back. The route you will take; the one that you won't. How you will pay...

Life doesn't only happen. Life happens in narrative, upon narrative, upon narrative.

It can be exhausting, I think. This storytelling requirement of being alive can exhaust a person's capacity to make up other kinds of stories.

For now it has surely exhausted mine.

Often, at readings, at talks, someone will ask me something along the lines of: "What do you do when you can't write?" More and more my answer is, *I do something else.* I know there are people for whom the better approach is to develop strict habits, write every day, even if nothing "useful" comes out; but for me, that is when the metaphor I am living shifts from feeling bearable—this hollow that eventually, probably will refill—to being untenable: the attempt to make it happen, the pushing, as if the problem were not an absence of material but an absence of force.

Force does nothing for me.

When I write, I am a woman possessed, aflame, obsessed. When I write, it feels as though I have taken the drug nature designed especially for my addiction, mine alone. When I write, I am only half in my "real" life. I am in an altered state of consciousness, believing that what I make up matters as much as anything else; and at moments, matters more. When I write, I am crazily in love.

I cannot force being crazily in love. I can only hope for the insanity to revisit me one day.

And try to enjoy these calm moments before the hollow next fills.

Acknowledgments

I am deeply grateful to Victoria Barrett and to Engine Books for welcoming this collection into the company of all those magnificent books they publish, and also for invaluable support and keen editorial guidance.

A very special thanks to the members of the late great blog *Beyond the Margins*, where many of these essays first appeared. I loved being part of that team of writers writing about writing. I learned so much from them all, especially from my dear friends Kathleen Crowley, Randy Susan Meyers, Nichole Bernier, and Juliette Fay. They taught me, through example and with lots of laughs, what kind of writer I want to be—not what I want to write, but who I want to be while I write.

My agent Henry Dunow is a source of endless wisdom, humor, and friendship. And I cannot imagine how I could have started writing and stuck with it without my once teacher, still mentor, and always friend Steven Schwartz.

Thank you to all my students, from whom I learn continually, and to the many writer friends and admired authors who are my teachers. And thank you to all the readers who have engaged with my work. It is an incalculable privilege to be part of your reading life.

My mother and my brothers have given me the extraordinary gift of encouraging me to write honestly about my late father, and about the many complexities of my relationship with him. I am fortunate to have family who understand why doing so matters so much to me, and who support this exploration of mine.

Anyone who has read this book knows I have a lot for which to thank my children, Elizabeth, David, and Annie. And I do thank them, with love, with homemade challah, with The Meal, with almond cookies, with amaretto pound cake—and with all that implies.

And thank you, Richard, always and endlessly. This is, in many ways, a love letter to you—as is everything I write.

Most of these essays have been individually published, often in somewhat different forms, and with different titles. Many thanks to these print and online publications: *The New York Times Magazine;* the *Chicago Tribune; Psychology Today, One True Thing; Psychologies Magazine; The Quivering Pen; Hunger Mountain; Gulf Coast Review; Bloom*; and of course, again, *Beyond the Margins.*

About the Author

ROBIN BLACK is the author of the story collection, *If I loved you, I would tell you this*, a Finalist for the Frank O'Connor Story Prize, and named one of the best books of 2010 by the *San Francisco Chronicle* and the *Irish Times*; and the novel *Life Drawing*, long listed for the Flaherty-Dunnan First Novel Prize, the Folio Prize, and The IMPAC Dublin Literary Award, and named one of the best books of 2015 by NPR. Her numerous essays and stories can be found in such publications as the *New York Times Magazine*, *One Story*, *O Magazine*, and the *Chicago Tribune*. She lives with her family in Philadelphia, and has taught most recently at Bryn Mawr College, as the Distinguished Visiting Writer, and in the Brooklyn College MFA Program.

CPSIA information can be obtained at www.ICGtesting.com
Printed in the USA
BVOW02s0005050316

439177BV00004B/17/P